Trailblazer in Flight

Britain's First Female Jet Airline Captain

Yvonne Pope Sintes

edited by Graham M Simons

Pen & Sword
AVIATION

First Published in Great Britain in 2013 by
Pen & Sword Aviation
an imprint of
Pen & Sword Books Ltd
47 Church Street, Barnsley, South Yorkshire S70 2AS

ISBN 9781783462674

A CIP catalogue record for this book is
available from the British Library.

Typeset in 10/12pt Palatino
by GMS Enterprises

Printed and bound in England by
CPI Group (UK) Ltd, Croydon, CR0 4YY

Pen & Sword Books Ltd incorporates the Imprints of Pen & Sword
Aviation, Pen & Sword Family History, Pen & Sword Maritime, Pen & Sword
Military, Pen & Sword Discovery, Wharncliffe Local History, Wharncliffe
True Crime, Wharncliffe Transport, Pen & Sword Select, Pen & Sword
Military Classics, Leo Cooper, The Praetorian Press, Remember When,
Seaforth Publishing and Frontline Publishing.

For a complete list of Pen & Sword titles please contact
PEN & SWORD BOOKS LIMITED

47 Church Street, Barnsley, South Yorkshire, S70 2AS, England
E-mail: enquiries@pen-and-sword.co.uk
Website: www.pen-and-sword.co.uk

Trailblazer in Flight

Britain's First Female
Jet Airline Captain

Contents

ACKNOWLEDGEMENTS

I would like to gratefully thank all the people who have helped and encouraged me.

Firstly, without the bullying of Graham Simons and the backing up of his wife, Anne this book would not be here. I also wish to thank Laura Hirst and all at Pen & Sword for their faith and patience!

Captain Leslie Gosling, BOAC started everything off by suggesting I became a flying instructor and my instructor husband, Eric Pope, agreed.

Captain 'Jock' Hunter with the Civil Aviation Flying Unit became my mentor, his kind wife, Betty putting me together again when necessary.

Despite prejudice, Captain Charles Argles of Morton Air Services enabled me to become a commercial pilot - he said it was because I was mad enough to go on their night paper flights!

However, it was Captain Bob Atkins who having accepted me as a pilot with Dan-Air, enabled me to become a jet captain.

Advice and encouragement for the writing of this book came from Captain Arthur Larkman and his wife Joy.

Captain Keith Moody was indeed kind enough to write the forward, having read the manuscript while on holiday! He and his wife Barrie kept my spirits up all the way, also giving sound advice.

I am very grateful for the interest of all my friends, including Rosemary and Derek Joyce, ex Air Traffic Controllers who have checked through my manuscript and have never ceased to encourage me. Other friends Berry Hudson and Maureen Sterling have helped with photocopying and my grandson Lewis Pope with scanning to make sure. I cannot thank my daughter-in-law Barbara Pope enough for transcribing my manuscript on to her computer in order to make it acceptable and for doing much behind the scenes.

I cannot thank everyone individually, but hope that they will all feel it was worthwhile - the support and understanding of my own family being the most important.

Finally,special thanks to my son Jon for his practical help and my grand-daughter Samantha for her assistance.

FOREWORD

Captain Keith J Moody (Ret'd)

When I started my flying career as a Pilot in the fifties, I was pleasantly surprised to find myself flying with two women pilots from time to time. These ladies were used on short contract and were ex-Air Transport Auxiliary Pilots from World War II. They did a magnificent job delivering all types of aircraft including fighters and bombers from the aircraft factories to Royal Air Force airfields.

Following on, Yvonne started as a flying instructor. Then, as the first female Ministry civilian Radar Controller, where the ability to think things through clearly was essential, she showed the characteristic determination to succeed, which remained with her even though the chauvinistic attitude of many of her compatriots initially made life difficult for her.

Yvonne Pope Sintes began airline work as a Hostess with British Overseas Airways, learnt to fly with their Airways Aero Club and ended as a Senior Jet Captain with Dan-Air Services, the first woman in Britain to become an Airline Jet Captain.

In 1964, having gained experience and flying hours on the Dakota doing night paper flights, Yvonne managed to persuade Morton Air Services to employ her as a full time First Officer and her flying career 'took off'!

Having overcome considerable opposition to the hiring of women pilots and also personal tragedy in the death of her first husband the day following the birth of their second son, this lady perpetuates the spirit of the British Air Transport Auxiliary and American Women Air Force Service Pilots.

In 1974, Yvonne received the Whitney Straight Award for her Services to Aviation – recognition of a fight well fought and won!

These days, Yvonne is held in well deserved high esteem and affection by her peers in the aviation world, and personally, my admiration of her many achievements and successes has not diminished in any way over the years I have known her.

This is a fascinating and amazing story and well worth reading!

Just some of the places we visited - often only seeing the airports!

PROLOGUE

'We can't land there!'
'I think the Queen would understand.'

The fuel gauge had suddenly plummeted towards the empty mark – the only possible site was Windsor Great Park.

Before landing we made a dummy run to warn the strollers of our intention. Just before touchdown I shouted 'Mind the cakes!'

After rolling to a gentle stop, Eric visually checked the fuel tank, while I inspected the rear locker. The fuel was ample, there was no leak; the Tiger Moth gauge was up to its usual tricks, and the cakes were secure.

We thankfully took off and flew on to our destination, Denham, where, to our great relief, we found the icing on our wedding cakes to be completely undamaged!

An immediate phone call was made to the police in case the bemused onlookers had complained. Two days later we were married and flew away – to another unauthorized landing…

BRITISH EUROPEAN AIRWAYS

P.O. Box No. 7

Bealine House, Ruislip, Middlesex.   Telephone 01-845 1234   Telegrams BEALINE LONDON

OJ/JLS/P   15 August 1967

Mrs Y E Pope
Skyway
9 Lambs Crescent
Horsham
Sussex

Dear Mrs Pope

Thank you for your completed application form in respect of employment
as a pilot. I have to confirm our subsequent telephone conversation,
wherein I stated that it was not the present policy of BEA to employ
women co-pilots.

I promised, however, I would ensure your application was sighted by our
Flight Management, in view of your civil licence qualifications, but
I still have to advise you that the present BEA policy is as stated
to you on the telephone earlier this month.

I am sorry I cannot be more helpful, but would thank you for your
interest.

                    Yours sincerely

                    J L STEPHENSON
                    Senior Employment & Services Officer
                    Flight Operations Department

How British European Airways judged my chances of employment.

Chapter 1

Early and Wartime Years

It was a beautiful clear sunny day, early in the summer of 1939. I was standing in the garden behind our house watching the tree tops of our wood being rustled by a gentle breeze. I suddenly saw an aircraft climbing up over the trees. It was etched against the blue of the sky. From that moment, I knew I had to fly.

We lived in Purley, near Croydon Airport, from which my father flew on business to Europe. Each time we went to the airport, I became more fascinated by the different aircraft and more determined that when I left school, I would somehow earn enough money to learn to fly.

I was born Yvonne Elizabeth van den Hoek on the 8th September 1930 in Pretoria, South Africa, and was brought to England in 1936 when my father was made Overseas Manager of the South African Citrus Exchange. The eldest of three girls, I was a quiet, shy and serious child. I was also plump – and hated it. My ancestry include English, Scottish, American, Dutch and Huguenot, which helped when I later used the dogged elements of Scottish and Dutch to go on a drastic diet in order to be accepted as a stewardess – and so become airborne.

In the meantime, 1939 brought the outbreak of the Second World War. I remember standing in the sunshine outside our front door and hearing the solemn announcement on the 3rd September. I had no idea what it would involve, but had a feeling of sadness and foreboding.

Thinking that Purley, so close to Croydon Airport could be bombed immediately, good friends invited us to stay with them in their house in the New Forest. Their chauffeur collected us and drove very carefully. When held up by a long line of vehicles ahead, I was justly chided for saying 'My father just puts his car in flying gear and goes over the top!' I was reminded of this many years later.

Our stay in the New Forest seemed an unreal vacuum. Their older daughter heard of an Army Camp which had been set up nearby and, with a little trepidation, I joined her to serve tea and sandwiches to the soldiers. We felt as though we were doing a little to help.

My father, who had had to remain working in London, was

able to join us for my 9th birthday, but it was a very quiet one. No-one knew what would happen next.

When it became apparent that Croydon was not an immediate target, we returned home, became used to blackout curtains of an evening and were in turn issued with gas masks and ration books. Air raid shelters were dug out of the school grounds and I was told that when not used for emergency drills, the resourceful cook used them for cooling the jellies for lunch.

After Dunkirk, when invasion was feared imminent, it was decided that my mother would take her three daughters back to safety in South Africa. The ship which sailed from Southampton was packed to capacity with women and children and I had to help take care of several youngsters. The worst experience came at the end of the voyage when I was pursuing a small boy, whose mother was in the passport queue with mine.

Watched by my second sister, Toni, aged six, my three year old sister, Marcelle had swarmed up the railings behind my back and could have dived headlong into the water between us and the quayside. I rushed back and grabbed her just before she reached the top rail!

. . . .

As we had visited South Africa only two years previously, it was not all that strange to be back, yet I felt curiously isolated. We spent several months living a restricted life in various hotels in Pretoria and I did not like the local school. Who doesn't feel the same about a completely different one? At last my mother found us a comfortable rambling old house with a big garden and tall jacaranda and fir trees. We settled down for the next four years. We were able to change to St. Mary's Diocesan School, which was much more pleasant, and we stayed there for the longest consecutive time we ever spent in any one school. The Nuns were kind and most of the lay teachers good.

However, my thoughts were centred on the progress of the War. The first priority of the day was to listen to the 8 o'clock news, which often nearly made me late for School Assembly.

Early on I bought a book on aircraft recognition and was known to study it even walking along the pavement. I got known as Yvonne 'head-in-air!' I also had a magazine picture of 'Cats Eyes Cunningham' stuck to the corner of my bedroom mirror. He was my pilot hero.

Through my father's work he was able to visit us twice during those war years. I remember very vividly getting up early in the morning to meet the flying boat at Vaal Dam. It seemed so remote initially and then large and impressive as it approached the landing stage. These visits were very precious to us and we felt bereft when he had to return to England. I longed to go with him and felt a deep sense of resentment at being kept safely away from the war. I yearned to be a man old enough to be a fighter pilot.

All I could do to ease the frustration was to read more and more. I became fascinated by flying stories of the First World War and really lived them, I also devoured every 'Biggles' book I could lay my hands on. Captain W.F. Johns will never know what he achieved, though he did impair my knowledge of Geometry, as his most recently acquired book was often read under my desk lid!

This addiction was aided and abetted in a curious way. I awoke one night with a sudden sharp pain in my left knee, which persisted for nearly an hour. Fortunately, the problem was rapidly diagnosed by our kind and brilliant Jewish doctor. He immediately called in a bone specialist but, X-rays were delayed due to it being my turn to develop Chicken Pox – my poor mother! The pictures finally confirmed that the cartilage at the top of the femur had been flattened and this was grating against the sides of the hip joint, causing the acute pain. I had thumped it once too often by descending too rapidly off a bike and off exercise rails. Treatment consisted of winding elasticized bandage around the offending leg and hanging a sandbag on the foot in order to keep the leg extended and give the cartilage a chance to renew itself. It was not known whether I would walk normally again, the probability being that the left leg would be somewhat shorter than the right.

I was immobilised in bed for six months and on crutches for the following three months. During the time I was at home my bed was wheeled out onto the veranda each day and my mother, being a qualified school teacher, made sure I did the lessons sent to me by the school. Fortunately, kind friends brought me all the books requested from the Library.

It was a really great day when I was allowed to get up and try walking on crutches. As soon as I had mastered the art and regained some strength in my right leg, I was once again able to catch the early bus to school. But it took a little longer getting ready and for the time being there was no hope of hearing the end of the 8 o'clock news!

After three months another X-ray was taken and it was found that I had had the best recovery known. I was able to walk normally again the only difference being that my left leg was a little thinner than my right. I would never have dreamt that I would one day walk the Atlantic as a stewardess. I cannot thank the doctor, the specialist and my mother enough.

Swimming was, initially, the only sport I was allowed as it did not involve exerting weight on the limbs, but I was later able to use a bicycle. My father had refused to buy me one during his first visit to South Africa as he said that I would be looking at the sky more than the road. He was partially correct; if there was an aircraft anywhere, my sight would be focussed on it. However, I was able to borrow a bike to pedal the sixteen miles to an aerodrome outside Pretoria to see the very first Spitfire which had flown down to South Africa. It was worth it, even if I did have to eat my breakfast off the mantelpiece the next morning because of a tender bottom!

Unable to do gym I found myself sitting this class out with another girl who had damaged her knee. We were complete opposites but subsequently became very good friends. It was she who led this serious student into a water fight against another form, for which we were duly castigated by the Mother Superior. However we made up for it by going to see the film 'Eagle Squadron', after which we had to have one of our own – and several intrepid adventures. Our escape from Germany was, however, put on hold when we temporarily lost her mother's car keys!

Sadly, her father, a veterinary Surgeon, was drowned when his ship was torpedoed on its way to India. I greatly admired the way Nancy coped with his death, but it meant that her mother, Mrs Howie, had to move her family to Cape Town and we were only able to follow nine months later. Those months were miserable. In between studying and letter writing, I climbed more frequently up into my eyrie in the fir tree, where I could read without interruption. The pressure to come first, second or, at worst, third in class became too much and I pretended to be ill. It didn't work – I should have known better – and the exams were sent home for my mother to invigilate! Little did I realise that I would spend the rest of my life making up for it. I eventually followed a career which necessitated taking exams every six months. Life will always catch up with you!

Chapter 2

First Flights and Family Break-ups

When it was, at last decided that we should move to Cape Town to await the end of the War, we found accommodation in a hotel in Sea Point, the other side of Table Mountain to where Nancy lived. We were only able to meet up over weekends. She had settled well and remained ebullient and confident. I was still quiet and serious.

The Government School to which I went had been denuded of most of its good teachers by the War, the exception being the brilliant History teacher, who taught it as a fascinating story. She kept discipline by using a few well chosen words, which made any offender feel uncomfortable and others keen to continue with the story. I still remember something of the Renaissance Period! Unfortunately basic maths had not been well taught by my previous teacher, who was unable to keep discipline or impart her knowledge easily. Here things went from bad to worse. When I was awarded 16% for a maths exam, all I could do was laugh weakly, having possibly come third from the bottom!

One very good idea was, however, instigated by the Head. She made us sit on the floor after Assembly on Mondays to listen to stirring music such as Fingal's Cave and the Ride Of The Valkeries. It was a good way to start the week, and began an interest in music I loved.

Victory in Europe came finally on the 8th May 1945. There was a tremendous feeling of relief, but at the same time unease, as the War against Japan still continued.

After what had seemed an endless year spent looking longingly over the sea at a distant horizon, we were at last able to return to England in a Union Castle ship, still in troopship configuration. Nancy's eldest sister was also travelling with her baby to rejoin her English husband. I kept an eye on the baby whilst Mary took her turn for meals, and was invited to visit them in Newcastle when Nancy came on holiday. Many years later they kindly put me up during my flying training as a Captain on the Avro 748.

Also on board was Virginia McKenna, who via the film 'Born Free' and her animal sanctuaries has done such wonderful work with the big cats and other maltreated animals the world over, saving them from extinction. She had been at the same school as Nancy, where I had seen them both in an end-of-term play. I would have been honoured to have her as a passenger any time.

The white rocks of The Needles finally loomed out of the early mist on that February morning in 1946. It was a typically cold damp day, but our train journey was enhanced by the delicate beauty of the outlines of the naked trees and the variety of the muted greens.

We returned to our house and school, Commonweal Lodge in Woodcote Village, Purley, and the family soon settled into the rather austere post-war pattern of life in Britain.

We were fortunate in being able to watch the Victory Parade from the balcony of South Africa House in Trafalgar Square. It was very impressive, but for me, saddened by the thought of all the lives lost, as is every Armistice Day ceremony.

During the voyage from South Africa my mother had persuaded a poor soul to attempt to coach me in Algebra. Whilst in the army, Neville Mapham had rebuilt the radio station in Rome and was on his way to take a degree in Civil Engineering at the University of London. He was very patient, but too well qualified. Having missed out on the basics, I was sadly unable to absorb his well intentioned efforts. However, he continued over weekend breaks when he came down to Purley to listen to classical music, which he also loved. He made me work through exam examples which I memorized. I eventually passed my Matric – not really knowing how!

I'm told that a Dutch ancestor, a gifted organist, was invited by President Kruger to come to South Africa after the Boer War. Suffice to say that both my parents loved classical music. My mother played the piano and my father, the violin, in the University Orchestra and local cinema. I started to learn the piano but was not very good. On returning to England my favourite piece became the Funeral March, and my poor mother, much as she disapproved, used to long for the time to switch on the radio for Dick Barton Special Agent! My sister Toni (Antoinette) was much better than I was, and my youngest sister, Marcelle, later learned the violin. I decided that I much preferred listening to other people playing really well, and was fortunate enough to be able to go to many London concerts and later, Opera and Ballets. I sat on newspapers in the 'gods' of the Albert Hall on many occasions! Our upbringing gave us an abiding love of music.

The most significant landmark of that period happened quietly and without warning. I was invited to spend a fortnight with friends of my father in Gothenburg. I was duly seen off at Tilbury on a brand new Swedish ship. The décor was so beautiful that I longed to have someone with whom to share my pleasure and appreciation. After a very interesting and enjoyable first week spent sight-seeing, my father joined us and we were able to spend a few days sailing round the nearby islands. Almost everyone had a boat. The daughter, Ingrid, and I then visited Stockholm. We travelled by train and, after a wonderful three day stay touring the 'Venice of the North', returned to Gothenburg by AIR! I couldn't believe it when my father told us to cancel our rail tickets and fly back!

That flight on an S.A.S. Skymaster remains almost unreal. My complete absorption and assimilation of every precious moment, high above the snow white clouds in the glorious sunshine, was so intense that time both stood still and yet flashed by. It was all that I had ever imagined it to be.

I was so obviously entranced that my father capitulated completely and allowed me to fly back to England as well. For once I managed to overcome my innate shyness and ask the pilots of the BEA DC 3 if I could possibly look at the cockpit after we had landed. I remember being completely fascinated by all the instrumentation and, surprisingly, not too unduly overawed.

A third flight completed the hat-trick that year, a pleasure trip over London in a Proctor from Croydon. Having progressed down the scale in size, I was so absorbed in the greater sensation of flight that I didn't really realize that the pilot was a woman this time. I accepted her as such, and it was only years later that I was delighted to tell that pilot, Monique Agarzarian, a wartime ferry pilot, of this encounter. I will always remember how she swooped down to show us our house, garden and woods!

The feeling of anti-climax which followed a return to mundane every-day life was both hard and inevitable. This was intensified by the break-up of my parent's marriage. I tried desperately to understand both sides.

Having sensed that something was wrong during our war years stay in South Africa, I had run away from home in the hope of bringing them together, but I now realized that the situation had become too serious and that things were beyond repair. However, the divorce was really traumatic. I was almost glad that my Matric exams were pending. I tried to lose myself in studying really hard, with the result that I achieved the required marks in most subjects, the exception being in English Composition. I was more fortunate in the November when I was able to write about an imagined flight through a turbulent thunderstorm, expanding on one of the exam choices. Years later I read almost my exact words in a book!

Having inherited a gift for languages from my father, I then decided that in order to learn to fly I would have to qualify for some kind of job which would earn me enough money for the lessons, wishfully thinking of using my school-girl French in the Diplomatic Corps! My mother had always wanted her daughters to have the opportunity of a University education, having so enjoyed it herself. There were no vacancies available at appropriate English Universities that coming year so I decided to try a South African one instead which would enable me to accompany my mother and sisters back to Pretoria. I wanted to see them safely settled after the divorce was made absolute. I hoped to return to England when qualified.

It was a very sad little party that once again set sail from Southampton at the end of 1947, just before Christmas.

Chapter 3

Attempt To Start A Career

On arrival at Cape Town, my mother and two sisters took the train up to Pretoria. I remained behind to await the arrival of my dog 'RAF', a mixture of Alsatian and Collie, who was greatly loved by one and all. He had had to travel with friends on a following ship.

It was the height of the summer so our train journey was dusty and hot. He had to travel in the guard's van so I jumped down at every stop to encourage him and make sure he had enough water and food.

We returned to live in the house where I was born – it had not been available during the war. One of my memories was of our lovely Alsatian 'Vicky' with whom I had been brought up. She was very gentle, but would prevent strangers from entering by standing up on her hind legs and putting her front paws on their shoulders. They remained immobile until the Master or Mistress gave permission for them to proceed!

My sisters returned to St. Mary's Diocesan School, where my mother later taught her favourite subjects, Science and Geography. It must have been very difficult for her, but fortunately, they were all able to catch up with all our relations and friends.

To start at Rhodes University, I had to take another long train journey down to Grahamstown, situated inland from the south coast. Although some of my wartime school friends had preceded me I felt very isolated. It is surprising how quickly I tired of the white sun beating out of a steel blue sky and longed for a little white cloud to break the monotony!

My two major subjects, English and French, did not come up to expectations. I only really benefited from some lectures in psychology, German – taught by a gentle Austrian with a soft accent – and typing, the last being the most useful!

Being so far away, I was unable to help my mother and two

sisters. Indeed, I became the 'black sheep' as I saw both sides of the divorce. During the holidays the only useful thing I possibly achieved was proof-reading the Wartime History of the South African Sixth Division, being compiled by their Intelligence Officer, the husband of a friend who had shared our home during the war. I worked from 8am to 4pm, leaving little time for recriminations.

The only fun thing at University was singing in the chorus of a production of *'Oklahoma'*, whilst the best thing was learning from a good-looking senior ex-Service student that to apologise openly when wrong was mature. I also learned to cope on an allowance of £5 per month!

Friends of relations, who were living in Grahamstown, were kind to me and invited me to their home for the occasional meal. It was good to be in a tranquil atmosphere with a happy family. Nevertheless, I became more and more depressed. I felt I was useless to my own family and not achieving anything worthwhile at University – neither they nor I had heard of a University Air Squadron!

Slowly I began to realise that I was not cut out for a Batchelor of Arts degree. Although the idea of a Foreign Office post had intrigued me, I didn't relish the thought of all the office work involved. Neither did I share my mother's vocation for school teaching, although I do admit that I later found flying instructing very satisfying.

During a phone call from my Father, he suggested that I should join him and my step-mother, Nan, in London. I accepted, realizing that this was my only hope of achieving anything with my life – and left without returning to Pretoria.

I arrived back in England on November 11th 1948, having figuratively burnt my boats, and feeling a complete failure after completing only one year at Rhodes. A warm welcome awaited from my Father and Nan, whom I had briefly met before leaving for South Africa. The day was a golden one and the drive though the autumn countryside was beautiful. However, I felt emotionally numb and remained so for a couple of years. With Christmas approaching I wanted to earn some money with which to buy presents and gladly accepted the offer of a job sorting out competition entries for a woman's magazine. Walking to work the first morning I noticed a Royal Air Force

Recruitment Office. I called in at lunchtime the following day but, alas, the Air Force would not, at that time, think of teaching women to fly – and I certainly wasn't interested in a ground job!

My magazine work lasted into January when a family friend offered me a temporary job of junior copy typist with his tin importing company, a scanty knowledge of typing being my only asset. He was very kind, but I soon realised that I definitely did not enjoy office work. As the junior I had to go out to buy the cakes and make the tea. The secretary disliked one of the poor men and would give him the smallest cake and the last cup of tea. When possible, I gave him the biggest cake and first cup of tea!

As an excuse to leave, I told my father that I felt my typing speed was inadequate. He immediately suggested a five-month secretarial course. I was not able to refuse!

However, prior to starting the course I was very kindly allowed to fly to Paris to spend a week with a pen-friend and her family during the Easter holiday. Thrilled as I was with the flight over, I suddenly noticed the stewardess and thought that if I could somehow become one, I would then perhaps be able to get the pilots to teach me how to fly. Although not a born nurse, I enjoyed looking after people and thought I might be able to cope.

On my return I put it to my parents, but their reaction was predictable – being an air stewardess could not be regarded as a career and a secretarial qualification would always be useful! I therefore had to get down to some really hard work. I must admit I did not enjoy it – so much so that I determined to get through it in the shortest possible time. I achieved the minimum qualifications in four months.

My first job was to help a friend of Nan's who ran a knitting agency which designed garments for magazines. It was not a success as far as I was concerned, but I hope I proved of some use. After a couple of months I decided that the lesser of two evils would be to retreat back to the secretarial college using the excuse, once again, that I needed to increase my speeds. Quite what I hoped to gain from this manoeuvre I'm not sure. I felt it would be a temporary escape from the commercial world and that then, by some miracle, I might find a job to do with aviation.

I achieved 50 and 120 words per minute in shorthand and typing and with Christmas approaching once more, helped out in a travel agency – a little closer to the air. Fate then took a hand in the proceedings. A family friend met the BOAC Public Relations Officer at a festive dinner and had the temerity to ask the best way of becoming a stewardess. He advised not writing a letter but going down personally to see the Recruitment Officer at Heathrow.

My family was persuaded to allow me to at least try. Very early in January I went down to London Airport to find the necessary office. I arrived promptly at 9am to be greeted by a dragon of a woman who asked me if I had an appointment. I said I was prepared to wait and did so until 5pm. I was then ushered in to see the Personnel Officer. Before I could sit down I was asked if I could cope with six men, had I done any catering, home nursing or first aid, and did I know Spanish? All I knew was a little French. I was also under age. One needed to be twenty-one and I still had eight months to go. He, nevertheless, suggested that if I accomplished all the above before my 21st birthday they might think of putting me on their training course. He also mentioned that there was a ten stone two pounds weight limitation. I was at that time twelve stone two pounds!

I went back to my long-suffering family with the news. My father thought of a catering course with Lyons, but found it would take a year. Whilst entertaining some guests at the Hungaria Restaurant in London, he bemoaned his fate to Joseph Vecchi, the owner/manager, who replied that they were always training staff and I could start the next day.

I began in the kitchen with the meat, chicken, vegetable and soup cooks, following on with the fish, hors d'oeuvre and dessert departments. The staff came from different parts of Europe but worked together harmoniously – the only British person was an Irishman! When I graduated to the restaurant itself, I was taught how to lay-up and wait at the tables by a kind Irish woman. After my first full day of lunch and evening duties, which also entailed running up and down the steps to the kitchen, I was unable to climb the five flights to my bed. I had to go up backwards on my bottom, following my father's example after he had damaged a knee in a storm on a cross-channel ferry.

Fortunately my legs became hardier as the days went by. However, I had my ups and downs. I scattered peas over the comedian Tommy Trinder whilst Joseph Vecchi was talking to him, and also nearly dropped an extra large pan of Crêpe Suzette into my step-mother's lap when my father came in with a business party of eight. I had never made Crêpe Suzette in my life, but was called over by the Maitre d'hôtel to do so. He blithely told me they would tell me how. Just prior to the exciting moment, one of the waiters kindly said he would find me a serviette for the handle, but before he could return another said 'light it' and I had to serve it immediately. The pan was heavy and the handle hot. I managed to stagger round the table, serving each in turn until I at last reached Nan when my strength nearly gave out! I escaped round a corner and stood there trembling. That dessert did not become a favourite!

After four weeks of waiting I was moved on to work behind the bar to learn the main drinks and cocktails. As I didn't start work until 11am and had time off between 3 and 6pm, I had been able to enrol with the Berlitz School of Languages to learn some Spanish. I also attended lectures on home nursing given by the St John Ambulance and finished with a week's concentrated course in first aid – after which I needed it!

In the meantime our family physician had prescribed Dr. Gray's diet which was working wonders. I lost seven pounds the first week, six pounds the second and then progressively less as I approached what should be my normal weight. The only trouble was that I became over-enthusiastic and cut out all starch so gumming up my works for a month or so. The potato is important as it provides mineral salts for the innards. I went down to nine stone ten pounds and our doctor was furious!

My parents did use it when they had done a little too much entertaining and I can recommend it. The diet was as follows:-

Breakfast: 1 egg, boiled, poached or scrambled with a little oil or 2 slices of grilled lean bacon with a tomato;

1 piece of toast with a scrape of butter and marmalade;

1 piece of fruit – apple, orange, pear or half a grapefruit;
Cup of tea or coffee without sugar.
Mid-morning: Drink without sugar.
Lunch: 2oz lean meat, fish, fowl or cottage cheese with as much green leaf vegetable or salad as possible, and one medium-sized boiled potato;

1 piece of fruit as above.
Afternoon tea: Cup of tea with lemon (no sugar) and one plain biscuit.
Supper: As for lunch but without potato.
Before bed: ½ cup of milk.
One glass of dry white wine per week!

Working at the Hungaria had helped greatly with the diet as the ingredients were easily available, but two months had passed and felt it was time to earn my keep. I wrote to the BOAC Personnel Officer advising him of my efforts but he replied, saying I was still too young and to re-apply when twenty-one. I therefore started the rounds of all the other airlines, personally and on foot!

Chapter 4

Air Stewardess

On my way home after a long and fruitless day, I almost walked past the Scottish Airlines Office. To my surprise they expressed interest in my qualifications. They were thinking of starting a new route from Prestwick to Northolt and might need more staff. They would be having a Board Meeting the following week and would let me know.

My parents quietly suggested that it might be a good idea to start with BOAC on the ground and then transfer to the air. To placate them I applied and was granted an interview during which I had to take a typing and shorthand test. As I hadn't used either for a while I failed! It was then suggested that they might be able to use me in the Personnel Department. I thanked them kindly but said I had another job pending. I learned afterwards that, once trained, it was difficult to change from one department to another.

I then plagued Scottish Airlines. My first phone call ascertained that the Board Meeting had been postponed for a day. My second elicited another delay. My third was met with the response "Oh for goodness sake, come and start in the office." So I did. This time I had to work their telephone exchange and sort out letters from would-be pilots. There were quite a few crossed lines and too many pilot applications!

The new route was approved, but it took a little while to implement. In the meantime I was asked to stand in for a Greek-speaking girl going on holiday. Scottish handled Olympic Airways and I had to take her place meeting Greek immigrants at Heathrow on their way to the States. I had to shepherd them onto coaches and explain that they would stay in a hotel overnight in London and be picked up again the following morning. I went back to the Hungaria and asked one of the Greek Cypriot waiters to translate the words for me. I learned them phonetically and was greatly relieved when it seemed that I was understood!

I was then transferred to Northolt where I was taught something about flight documentation, going on to check in passengers on the new scheduled and charter flights. However, I did not enjoy the pilots standing over me whilst I made out the necessary load sheets. On one occasion I made a mistake over the weight of a passenger's baggage. After he had passed through I found it was overweight and rushed after him. He merely replied that it was my mistake and I would have to pay the £6. This cost me one week's salary!

At last came my turn to fly. I was checked out on the safety equipment and procedures on the Dakota and initially flew supernumerary in the galley. The scheduled flight was from Northolt via Burtonwood to Prestwick where we night-stopped, returning the next morning. I was allowed to serve the passengers on the following flight and then let loose on my own.

The flight was via Bovingdon to Le Bourget with race-goers. To my chagrin, I forgot to uplift the trays so the passengers were served their food in boxes! We had from 11am to 6pm free in Paris so I was able to have lunch with friends I had met on holiday. It took so long that I barely had time to be rushed across the city on the back of a motorbike (in my sky blue uniform) to very briefly visit my pen-friend and her family. I only just made it back to the airport in time!

Then followed flights to Marseilles, Rome, Athens, Geneva, Malta, Cairo, Benghazi, Tripoli, Gatwick, Jersey, Le Bourget again and Dublin. Unfortunately one does not usually see much of the places to which one flies other than the airports, which are on the whole similar. Even when staying overnight, time has to be spent in making sure the aircraft is secure and in organizing the next day's catering, the cleaning and flight documents, such as weather forecasts. Thus it was, that when night-stopping Athens, there was only time for a late supper, and all we saw of the Parthenon was from the taxi on our way back to the airport!

However, we did at least have time for a swim in a rocky Mediterranean creek before breakfast in Malta, and we were able to have tea on the terrace of the famous Shepherd's Hotel when in Cairo for a night, though we were not allowed to go into the city due to rioting!

Some sights always remain. I will never forget my first flight to Ireland. We came into land at Dublin just before sunset and the grass was an incredible liquid emerald green. On our way home the moon rising over the Welsh hills was truly breathtaking.

Although I had enjoyed working with Scottish, I decided to try my luck again with BOAC. I had learned from some BEA personnel at Northolt that the two corporations subsidised a combined Flying

Club and that anyone employed by either of them was eligible to join. I wrote the day after my twenty-first birthday giving them my up-to-date details. I signed myself:

Yvonne van den Hoek – third time lucky?!

I was surprised by a phone call at 10 o'clock the following morning summoning me to an interview, during which I was asked the distance to Rome and whether I liked children. Remembering childhood experiences of separating my warring sisters and looking after those children on the ship, I said "I loved them" – and was accepted!

I started their training course in the October. It was held in an old building in Southall which was shared with International Aeradio who specialized in maps for aviation. Little did I know that my husband-to-be had once worked for them as a draughtsman!

It seemed that some of the instructors were determined to show us that the job was not a glamorous one, but the two girls on the course were given a day up in London to be taught how to make up and use the Elizabeth Arden kit, individually issued, for use in the aircraft rest rooms. These kits provided cleansing liquid and make-up for the female passengers.

We did indeed practice serving a seven course meal in an aircraft mock-up, but apart from the safety equipment, the most interesting lectures were the ones on Arctic and Desert Survival. The cabin crew are there primarily for the safety of the passengers, in order to evacuate them as quickly as possible in the event of an accident. Aviation law requires a minimum number according to the size of aircraft and passengers carried.

After qualifying, my first rostered duty was as standby for the South American flight departing on Christmas Day. After checking in at Heathrow on Christmas Eve, I was transported to Dormy House, the BOAC rest house at Sunningdale, where I stayed overnight with some very subdued cabin and air crew. They would be away for at least ten days.

The standby crew was awakened earlier than the operating one to go to the airport to draw out the required equipment from stores for the out-going flight. They then had to check all the safety equipment on board and prepare the cabin, toilets and galley for departure. After breakfast the operating crew took over and we were allowed to stand down, but had to wait until at least thirty minutes after the aircraft had departed before we were released. It was good to be able to rejoin my parents for Christmas Dinner!

My first operational flight was to Rome, Beirut, Kuwait, Bahrain, Cairo Rome and London. East instead of West! The Argonaut Line steward stood behind me whilst I gave the briefing on departure from Heathrow. It had to be shouted over the noise of four Rolls Royce Merlin engines as we taxied out. I was very nervous at first but after the first sector, realized that I had looked after the thirty two passengers courteously on the Dakota on my own and would be able to care for the forty eight that the Argonaut carried. There were now three of us. The Chief Steward was in charge of the organization of cabin service and the ordering of stores en route, whilst the Second Steward looked after the galley.

My second flight was more enjoyable as we went to South America. The ex-British South American crews, who had been taken over by BOAC, were friendly and caring. Take-off from Heathrow was at 9am and the route was via Madrid/Lisbon or both, to Dakar with perhaps a tech-stop for fuel at Casablanca. Breakfast and two seven course meals were served with tea and drinks in between. We would usually arrive about 2am, reaching the rest house at 3am.

We slept ourselves out and remained there for three to four days, waiting for the next aircraft. Other than visiting the very dusty market in the town we spent most of the time on a lagoon-type beach, being driven there by a rickety old bus. In between swimming, we played cricket or read in the sun all day – there was no shade. We didn't know about the accumulation of sun causing skin cancer back then!

Attempting to sleep before taking on the next aircraft to Rio was difficult due to the proximity of an open-air cinema just opposite. However, I did learn to have breakfast at midnight and this stood me in good stead when I later flew night-paper flights. The flight across took approximately nine hours and we would arrive at Recife between six and seven in the morning local time, where the passengers and crew would have light refreshments in an already steamy dawn. Then another five hours on to Rio, where we could spend three to five days.

After a long three months, I was able to join the Airways Aero Club.

Chapter 5

Learning To Fly

On the 20th March 1952 I took the coach from London to Uxbridge and then bus to Denham. There I had to ask the way to the airfield. As I walked up the hill on the concrete road I was suddenly afraid that I might feel sick in a light aircraft. I had been very car-sick when young. But I also had the strange feeling that I was walking towards my destiny.

Luckily I was taken up in an open cockpit aircraft, a Miles Magister. The instructor flew it around gently. I didn't feel at all air-sick; I loved it and was completely fascinated. Shortly afterwards I had to fly to Rio again. This time the Captain was Leslie Gosling, who had been a wartime instructor. During the long night flight across the Atlantic, the navigator came back for a meal break. For something to say, I admitted that I had had my first air experience flight at Denham. He immediately said that he would tell the Captain. I protested; the cabin crew had been taught that a BOAC Captain was a God-like figure who we almost had to salute when he came aboard. He assured me that this one was different. Soon afterwards, to my amazement, I was invited to the cockpit and warmly told that I would be welcome to come up whenever I had a free moment. I was subsequently taught straight and level flying at 10,000 feet, aiming for small clouds on the Atlantic horizon. Fortunately the passengers were completely unaware that the stewardess was flying the aircraft!

Leslie Gosling loved flying so much that he also enjoyed instructing with the Airways Club and, on our return, taught me climbing and descending on a 'Maggie' – the Magister. Leslie was a born instructor. He became fascinated with aeroplanes at an early age and worked in hangars, helping clean aircraft in the hope of being taken up. His enthusiasm was rewarded with several flights and he obtained his Private Pilot's Licence at 16. After gaining his Commercial Licence and Instructor's Rating he joined the RAF as an instructor in 1939. Sent to Canada in 1941 to train pilots as instructors, he gained the highest RAF qualification: A1 – Excellent. When he returned to the UK he flew Lancaster Bombers until the end of the war, after which he joined BOAC. He became an Instrument Rating Examiner and Line Check Captain flying with new Captains to ensure that they knew the routes and procedures at each airport. Temporarily seconded to British South American Airways, he flew the Lancastrian, Avro York and Avro Tudor. After being involved with the Berlin Airlift in April 1949, he was posted onto the Argonaut, again with BOAC, which was how we met. He ended his 19 years with the Corporation as a Senior Captain and Master Pilot, having flown many well known VIP celebrities, including Prime Ministers. Apart from being a wonderful instructor, he was a warm, gentle and generous man. He and his attractive and practical wife, Kit, were to become very good friends and later Godparents to my children. It was he who suggested that I become a Flying Instructor!

....

In between flights to South America, I spent all my free time at Denham, to the despair of my step-mother who wanted to know why I couldn't be interested in Art or Museums?!

My main instructor was a tall, quiet and serious man called Eric Pope. I was in awe of him at first, but then began to appreciate his calm and efficient instruction. When he sent me solo, after eight and half hours, I was grimly determined to do everything correctly for him and landed with only a small bounce. Thrilled as I was, I didn't dare tell my family immediately. I waited until my father had to entertain some business friends at the Savoy Hotel in London and then told him in the middle of the dance floor! He seemed pleased but didn't dare say too much. I believe he would have liked to learn himself, but my step-mother had lost too many friends in the War. Sadly I was never allowed to take him up as Nan was afraid of losing both of us. In the meantime Leslie Gosling continued to encourage me and another Captain, 'Dutch' Holland, who had also been an instructor, would invite me into the cockpit when possible. They both tried to teach me Astro-Navigation – 'Dutch' with a stick in the sand on a beach near Copacabana, and Leslie up in Javari, a quiet haven supposedly constructed by a President for his mistress.

Leslie had heard of this refuge up in the mountains en route to San Paulo, when stuck in Rio one Christmas. He offered to take us up there during a five-day lay over. We accepted with alacrity and enjoyed the simple hotel with its balconies over-looking the 'man-made' peaceful lake surrounded by tropical vegetation. He and the navigator did their best to teach me the star constellations in the pure night skies but unfortunately I didn't remember many as I didn't have the opportunity to use them.

However, I did achieve my first solo on a horse, having only once ridden a donkey bare-back on a South African farm. The navigator lent me his spare trousers after the Skipper had hired some horses from Shangri-La, a nearby Hacienda. The others set off at a brisk walk which became a trot. Intent on catching up, mine decided to gallop and nearly chucked me head first into the lake! Fortunately it then settled down and we made it safely back to the Hotel. Despite slightly injured pride, that was one of the most pleasurable stay-overs we had. Sadly, no-one else thought of following suit.

BOAC had the top floor (the sixth) of the Serrador, at that time the tallest hotel in Rio, and the rooms had a wonderful view of the Harbour Bay, Sugar Loaf and Corpus Christi Mountains, but the city itself was a disappointment. The main streets had pot holes in the pavements and the side streets were awful. There was a rather tense, uneasy atmosphere in the city, which teemed with a polyglot of nationalities. I was told that if anyone had an accident, no-one would go to help for fear of being involved and indicted. On my very first day I found out that a nice girl shouldn't walk up even the main streets on her own. I was trying to find the office of my father's friend and hadn't been warned! Pretending I was married didn't deter amorous advances.

The famous Copacabana Beach had open sewers running through it and many of the hotels looked as though they needed a coat of paint. It was dangerous to bathe from the beach and we were told that a senior BOAC official had been drowned in a so-called safe area. Instead, we found an unpopulated and reasonable beach beyond it. However the nearest safe one was the small one, close to the centre of Rio, but it was very crowded. The official language of Brazil is Portuguese so my smattering of Spanish didn't help very much! Nevertheless we did manage to go up via the cable car to the top of the Corpus Christi and the views were fantastic. One night from my bedroom I saw the Statue of Christ illuminated between gaps in the fast moving cloud. It was truly ethereal.

Having seen the sights there was not much to do other than go to the beaches, but I was fortunate in that my father's friend introduced me to a family whose daughter was my own age and I was welcomed to their home at any time. It was a real haven and their kindness was greatly appreciated. I was able to wind down, relax and enjoy classical music. However, I became resentful of the time spent away from England and Denham; it could be ten days and up to three weeks if we went on to Buenos Aires and Santiago in Chile.

Having gone solo, I began to realize the freedom of being alone above the earth and how it diminished the size of problems on the ground, putting them into perspective. I longed to get on with my flying. I progressed a little more each time I went home and found that map reading was easier than Astro-Nav. The only problem was coping with the compass which tended to wander rather frequently. My first solo cross-country flights went quite well. However I misinterpreted a rail junction on my qualifying one and failed to realize that I was heading rather more towards the sun than having it on my left! Fortunately a large aerodrome suddenly appeared which should not have been there, so I swiftly back-tracked to the known junction and took the right-hand fork. Although duly chagrined, I was delighted to hear (at a much later date) that my instructor had had a similar experience – only the identifying letters in the signals square of his airfield were 'BF' – Bloody Fool!

Shortly afterwards I took my Private Pilots Test with the Chief Instructor. I passed everything except spinning. I was nervous and forgot to turn the Magister both ways to look below and all round for other aircraft before going into the spin. As well as feeling disgusted with myself I felt terrible about letting my instructor down. I had to do thirty minutes spinning with him before retaking the test the next day!

Later when I became an instructor myself, I drummed those necessary turns into my own pupils' heads and, indeed, while doing a Commercial Test dummy run for an RAF friend, was able to tell him that he would have failed for the same reason. As my father used to say, "It's all good experience."!

Chapter 6

Royal Air Force Volunteer Reserve

Fate once again intervened.

After obtaining my Private Pilot's Licence on the 31st July 1952, I learned that the Royal Air Force Volunteer Reserve had just reduced their qualifying hours from one hundred to fifty. I only had to pay for another 11 hours 25 minutes to be eligible. I was determined to obtain these as soon as possible, but had spent nearly all my salary each month on learning to fly. As a stewardess I earned a basic salary of £8.00 per week, which, with flying pay could bring me up to £11.00 when on long distance flight. Dual instruction cost £3.00 per hour and flying solo £2.50, but I also paid my parents £3.00 per week for my keep and had to add transport from London to Denham. My budget was very tight!

Incidentally, the RAFVR was formed in July 1936 to provide individuals to supplement the Royal Auxiliary Air Force which had been formed in 1925 by the local Territorial Associations. The AAF was organised on a Squadron basis, with local recruitment similar to the Territorial Army Regiments. Initially the RAFVR was composed of civilians recruited from the neighbourhoods of Reserve Flying Schools, which were run by civilian contractors who largely employed as instructors members of the Reserve of Air Force Officers, who had previously completed a four year short service commission as pilots in the RAF. Navigation instructors were mainly former master mariners without any air experience. Recruits were confined to men of between 18 and 25 years of age who had been accepted for part time training as Pilots, Observers and Wireless Operators. The object was to provide a reserve of aircrew for use in the event of war.

When war broke out in 1939 the Air Ministry employed the RAFVR as the principal means for aircrew entry to serve with

the RAF. A civilian volunteer on being accepted for aircrew
training took an oath of allegiance and was then inducted in to
the RAFVR. Normally the volunteer returned to his civilian job
for several months - sometimes longer - until he was called up
for aircrew training.

At the end of World War Two, the RAFVR was reconstituted
in 1947, and continued to act as a focus for individuals who had
a continuing obligation under the Acts, peaking in its activities
at the end of the 1950s.

Thanks to a three week trip to South America, I achieved the
extra hours towards the end of August and then, fortunately,
passed my Acceptance Test with the Commanding Officer of
Fairoaks, which was the R.A.F.V.R. training airfield in our area.
As a friend of the Chief Instructor of the Airways Club, he
offered to fly me back to Denham. En route he asked if I liked
aerobatics. I had never done any but, of course, said 'yes' and
was treated to the most superb display. It seemed so effortless
that only the earth appeared to move! I was determined to try
some myself. Harold, a friend of mine, was equally enthusiastic
so we went up in a 'Maggie' armed with the handbook 'Teach
Yourself to Fly'. We opened it at the appropriate page and read
the instructions to each other in turn. Our loops were rather
ragged but, nothing daunted, we continued with attempts at
rolls. The poor De Havilland Gipsy Major engine, however, was
not impressed!

Our efforts had produced low oil pressure and we had to
make a precautionary landing at the nearest airfield, Booker
near High Wycombe. We ignominiously took a taxi back to
Denham. When we arrived back, Eric Pope had left us a
drawing of the cartoon character 'Chad' on the blackboard:
'Wot, no oil pressure?!'

I continued to fly at Denham in between R.A.F.V.R. flying.
Looking at beautiful countryside through a friend's window, I
suddenly realised that I loved Eric. I had fallen in love with my
quiet 'serious' instructor. My first concern was that he might
be married. After my parents sad divorce, I was not going to
interfere with anyone else's marriage. Judicious questioning
revealed that he was not married, but seemed to be going out
with someone. I had to wait to see...

He too had been accepted into the R.A.F.V.R. and we were

both required to do our annual training that autumn. Unfortunately we had an engine failure just prior to the reporting date.

The Airways Club had very recently taken delivery of a brand new Auster Aiglet. There were jokes about who would be the first to 'prang' it. We had that dubious honour! As part of the familiarization, we had been doing several 'circuits and bumps' – opening up the throttle to go round again after landing to save time in taxiing back. The men and I had also had difficulty with the new flap mechanism which was stiff and awkward. Eric decided on one more circuit, but this time the power started to fail as soon as we became airborne. Eric took over and managed to nurse it over the tree tops. We were, of course, taking off towards the most wooded area due to the wind direction. When he said "door open" and "full flap", the flaps came down without a problem! We touched down in a small field which was divided from another by barbed wire. We didn't even notice it but were brought to a sudden unexpected standstill when the second field gave way to a bunker which had been a small quarry prior to being incorporated into the local Golf Course. The undercarriage splayed out and the propeller stopped abruptly!

We shot out of our respective aircraft doors, only to be rapidly brought up short by the leads of our headsets which were plugged into the central pedestal. We hastily released them and then stood at a respectful distance waiting for the aircraft to blow up! When it didn't oblige, Eric suggested that I should climb up to the nearby farmhouse to advise the Club. As I reached the top I surprised two golfers who had just passed through the bunker. Our arrival had been silent and I was in my V.R. flying suit – they probably thought I had come from Mars!

I didn't dare tell my parents but friends read about it in the papers. Due to over-sleeping, my parents hadn't had time to read through their Telegraph so had gone to work none the wiser. However, their caring friends kept phoning all day and I wasn't quick enough to put the phone down when they walked in that evening. They were furious! I learned too late that reporters went round the police stations touting for a story. Even my next BOAC crew read about it in Rome. Sadly white lies of omission don't work!

The Aiglet was sent back to Austers at Rearsby, where it had been manufactured, but they found nothing wrong with the engine, so the pilots were blamed. It was thought that I had opened up the mixture control with the throttle but then it was discovered that the control wasn't even linked up. A year later, after two more power failures, it was found that one side of a box was not correctly soldered and when the engine became hot, it allowed air in which weakened the mixture causing loss of power. We felt better after that!

In the meantime Eric was held back by the accident paperwork and I had to start the R.A.F.V.R. training on my own. I found digs in a village near Fairoaks and hired a bicycle. After a hasty wash in a cold bathroom and a rushed breakfast, I would set off early to the airfield so that I stood a chance of being taken up on the weather check. If conditions were suitable I was often able to continue with the same aircraft instead of having to wait for one to be allocated. Ground instruction, which included Navigation and Meteorology, was interspersed with flying. I preferred being airborne, but exams had to be passed.

I found instrument flying fascinating. Amber screens were positioned so that the trainee could not see out of the cockpit and would have to learn to fly solely on instruments. I will never forget the feeling of complete surprise when the wheels of my Chipmunk touched down on the runway at Odiham after the R.A.F. Controller had talked me all the way down to a blind landing.

After proper instruction, I practised aerobatics over the Hog's Back between Guildford and Farnham. However, my first attempt at a loop through a little fluffy white cloud came out as a spiral dive. I hadn't yet learnt to fly upside down in cloud!

When Eric joined the course we went for long silent walks after flying finished for the day.

Whilst scuffing through the autumn leaves I learned that the friend he had been helping had finally joined the man she wished to marry, who had been waiting for a divorce. When I was asked to baby-sit by an instructor, I tentatively asked Eric if he would like to help me. During that evening in the instructor's caravan we discovered that we had quite a lot in common, including a love of classical music and a similar sense of humour.

....

On returning to the South American route I found I was becoming more and more disenchanted with my work. I enjoyed looking after people and making them comfortable, but businessmen on expenses were very demanding and wished to be attended to regardless of the needs of other, perhaps infirm, passengers. Members of the Nobility were the most appreciative and courteous, but some South Americans were very uncertain about the care of their children. On one occasion, the Captain, fortunately a family man, had to come back to reassure a distraught mother that her infant did not need a penicillin injection because it was hot. All that was needed was the removal of excess clothing! However, the same Captain would have been horrified to know that the stewardess and second steward were quite often standing in the galley on landing finishing off the washing-up!

I increasingly longed to be up front in the cockpit and wrote to Eric from Rio, wistfully asking for help. He met me on my return – and asked me to marry him! I couldn't believe it, and wanted to be sure. He next proposed in the air after Christmas but, although desperately in love, I wanted him to be completely certain. We had to wait until New Year's Eve, when listening to Beethoven's Seventh Symphony, he asked me again. This time I said jokingly that he would have to do gown on his knees. When he did, I couldn't refuse!

When we told our families, Eric's mother wept with happiness, but his aunt didn't think I was good enough for her brother's son. My step-mother thought that most pupils became infatuated with their instructors and that it was a passing fad. She had hoped that I would marry the doctor's or bank manager's son. My father only asked him, "Do you know what you're taking on?"!

We decided on a very small wedding in the lovely old church at Harefield which we had seen from the circuit at Denham. I chose the first day of Spring and Eric put a suitcase in a room in the village to qualify. I gave my notice and was only sorry to say goodbye to our BOAC rest house in Chile. It was in the foothills of the Andes, away from the city of Santiago, and had an English-type orchard garden with a stream flowing through it. The atmosphere was very peaceful and we had all longed to have more than twenty-four hours there, but didn't suffer the hoped-for engine failure during my time. However, the kind housekeeper ordered me some really warm double-sided blankets, similar to those used in the Guest House and they indeed came in very useful over the years. On the return trip they were stowed in any available corner on the Argonaut!

Whilst flying through a southern valley of the Andes, my last view of the snowbound peaks through broken cloud, almost at our level, was unforgettable. It was somehow more impressive than when over the peaks in clear air. From the good friends in Rio, I had been given a decorative rolling-pin. This had an inscription on it in Portuguese, which when translated said 'Master of the House am I, but the person who gives the orders is my Wife'. Just as well Eric didn't understand Portuguese!

We usually had several days off after a three week trip, thirty-six hours normally being the minimum. However, this time I was called out almost immediately to do a trip to Beirut with Service families. Towards the end of the flight, one of the poor mothers was airsick so I offered to change her baby. The tin of talcum powder refused to open so I took it and the bare-bottomed baby up to the Navigator. He also had difficulty, but with brute strength pulled the top off completely, scattering powder all over his charts. We beat a hasty retreat! On arrival at the hotel, I was so tired I slept for nearly the whole thirty-six hours, only waking a couple of times for an omelette. It was time to leave.

Chapter 7

The Wedding

Early in 1953 it was decided that the Airways Aero Club would move to Croydon Airport. During time off Eric and I started looking for possible accommodation. After abortive enquiries and forays in miserably cold weather, we hit upon the idea of a caravan. Even so we saw few sites in the slushy snow that were reasonably close to the airport. Some things are just not meant to be.

Three weeks before the wedding we were spared further efforts. Eric was made redundant – the Club was being restructured! He decided to start studying for the Commercial Pilot's Licence as soon as possible, and bought the Correspondence Course from Avigation.

We determined to go ahead regardless and redecorated his attic bedroom as a bed-sit. I also persuaded him to help me make the wedding cakes and accepted his mother's suggestion of taking them down to Bournemouth to be iced by friends who were experts. Not having a job would at least mean that we did not have to hurry back from our honeymoon!

We wanted to spend the first week in the country so, after delivering the cakes, used the next day to reconnoitre. Despite several bus trips and long walks between villages, we had no luck. Country pubs had stopped taking guests. All we achieved was a soaking from a thunderstorm. Reluctantly we provisionally booked into a hotel in Blandford. However, during my last flight, Eric found an unusual advertisement on the back of a Railway Guide book. It gave details of 'God's Tryst Guest House', a small homestead in Compton Abbas near Salisbury. After phoning we thankfully decided to book in for a week. Good friends had offered us the use of their cottage near Newbury for the first weekend of our honeymoon.

I found a wedding dress in a good second-hand shop at the bottom of Oxford Street for £5, after which I had £5 left in my

bank account. Thank goodness Eric had saved a little money
during the War. He invited Keith Johnstone, a good friend in
the RAF at Valley, to be our best man. They had learned to fly
in different ways, having shared their interest in flying over
many years. Eric had been involved with aircraft production at
the beginning of the War so had not been released to join the
Air Force, but had managed to do so on gliders in the Air
Training Corps.

Inez Kennard, a friend of mine, was arriving from South
Africa the day before the wedding so was persuaded to help
me. Our cakes had to be collected from Bournemouth so I went
down by train, but at the last minute Eric was able to fly a Tiger
Moth to Christchurch. After returning – via Windsor Great Park
– the beautifully iced cakes were deposited in the Denham Club
House where the reception was to be held.

I met Inez and another nurse friend off the boat train in
London on the morning of the 20th. They wished to visit South
Africa House and do some shopping prior to joining me before
3pm to go down to Harefield. They lost themselves! I waited
as long as I dared, but then had to make my solitary way,
armed with flowers my father had bought in Covent Garden
that morning. As the 21st March was in Lent, the Reverend
Connor had kindly suggested we could provide our own. The
Vergeress had agreed to meet me at 5pm that evening.

The sun had set by the time I approached the Church and a
mist was forming. I felt very alone. Suddenly a familiar figure
appeared through the gloom walking towards me. Eric was
supposed to be London meeting Keith, but his train had been
delayed. He had come to help in the Church. It was so good to
do it together.

Afterwards, we went our separate ways to pick up our errant
friends and finally met up at the Club House at 10pm. Keith
and Eric were staying there, but we were booked into a pub in
Harefield.

Just as we finished putting the cakes together a party turned
up unexpectedly and stayed until nearly 3am! The owner had
offered to run us down to our accommodation so I had
dismissed our taxi. No other was available, so we had to wait
until the party was over. I phoned to advise that we would be
late – but didn't realise just how late!

When we finally arrived I had to plead on my knees in the gravel, saying "Please, please let us in – I'm going to be married this morning!" The wife took pity on us and showed us up the back stairs.

We awoke to a foggy cold morning. I felt emotionally and physically exhausted and thought "this can't, just can't be my wedding day – we're not going to be able to fly away and will have to go by train!"

A hot bath helped, but it wasn't until I received a phone call from Eric that I felt things would be alright. However, I started shaking whilst my friends helped me dress. Being nurses, one of them bought me something from a nearby chemist. I remember only a slight tremble as I walked up the aisle. The sun came through in the middle of the Ceremony and the mist receded as we drove up the hill toward Denham.

After cutting the famous cake we changed into flying suits for our departure – to the dismay of my step-mother, a beauty expert. Unbeknown to us, the Auster Aiglet had secretly been decorated from nose to wing with white ribbons and 'Just Married' and 'Good Luck' chalked on either side of the fuselage. Fortunately aviation law forbade kippers to be attached to the exhaust!

Another flying instructor had been persuaded to fly as passenger to return the aircraft to Denham. I was allowed to do the take-off, but Eric took over for flying low over the guests. I then flew the aircraft to our destination, Welford near Newbury, but Eric did the landing. Towards the end of the run the aircraft did a sudden 90 degree turn to the left – Eric wasn't used to drinking champagne!

No sooner had we come to a halt when a furious little Austin Seven came rushing across the airfield with an equally furious officer in it. We did not know that Welford was still maintained by the RAF, not having seen any signs of life when we had previously reconnoitred. All we could do was apologise humbly and offer him a piece of wedding cake!

It had taken us half an hour to fly there and it took nearly the same time to walk to the nearest bus stop with our suitcases. The only bus for the next two hours arrived within ten minutes. It was our lucky day – especially as our only castigation was a 'Notice to Airmen' advising civil pilots that they really must not land at service airfields without prior permission!

When we reached Compton Abbas on the Monday, we were given a really warm welcome and greatly benefitted from its peace and tranquillity – God's Tryst was indeed a retreat. We spent the week exploring the beautiful Dorset countryside on foot – I, who had never walked any distance in my life. We eventually reached the Roman Remains near Dorchester, but had to take a taxi back to be in time for supper!

Because we both wore corduroy, I had proudly bought a corduroy skirt, we were initially taken for a couple of school teachers on holiday, but, when confetti secreted by a 'friend' in my suitcase was discovered in our waste paper basket our secret was out and our hostess was thrilled.

We then went on to stay with Eric's kind relation in the West Country, which we toured by bus. He had previously done so on a bicycle, using holidays to cycle from London. We went to Cheddar Gorge, Minehead, Porlock and Kilve, walking across its green cliff head, which for me had the most incredibly peaceful atmosphere. We were to return there.

Finally we had to return to reality, bidding our kind hosts a very grateful farewell.

Chapter 8

Marriage And
An Instructors Licence

Back at Ealing, Eric settled down to study, but was also invited to do some part-time instructing with a new club at Denham. His mother was very welcoming and kind. Not only did she offer any help possible, but also taught me how to fry chips! I had not previously enjoyed the soggy ones in newspaper, but soon joined Eric in appreciating his favourite – egg and chips, which helped us eke out his savings. We tried to manage on not more than £5 per week.

I did as much RAFVR flying as possible, getting up at 5am to catch the necessary train from London. I was eventually told that I had exceeded the hours allowed! It was worth it. I was building up the hours required for an Assistant Instructors Licence. I had not believed it when Leslie Gosling had said that a woman could be a flying instructor, and Eric had agreed with him.

Eric started giving me the course that April and despite the Husband/Wife relationship, he was again completely impartial. The only thing we argued about was the terminology. On paper his 'patter' seemed very stark and I wanted to soften it. He just said 'Wait until you have to shout it down a Gosport tube' (the rubber tube which joined the in-tandem cockpits of the Magister and the Tiger Moth). I learned my lesson, and soon reverted to the original. When possible I practised on the R.A.F.V.R.. Chipmunks, which I loved, and on any other aircraft available, including a tiny Dart Kitten, which was privately owned.

Sadly, the RAFVR was slowly being run down and the unit at Fairoaks was closed. Eric was honourably discharged, but I was transferred to Redhill where the Commanding Officer, Squadron Leader Lash, was also a Civil Examiner. After achieving the required hours I was able to take my test on the 14th September. Whilst checking the aircraft, the engineer casually mentioned that the C.O. had had a controlled crash the previous day. During a display, the aircraft had failed to recover correctly from a spin. It had flattened and he had made rather a dusty landing. (I afterwards learned that it was not his usual aircraft and did not respond in the accustomed way).

This information helped. I made quite sure that I was plenty high enough and looked very carefully each way before demonstrating my spin. I passed and was delighted to be able to start doing some part-time instructing at Denham. Although not a born school teacher, I really enjoyed teaching people to fly.

Shortly afterwards we had to make a private flight up to Keith and Mair's wedding in Wales on the 25th September, Keith having been the Best Man at our wedding. We flew up to Valley on the 24th, hiring a four-seater Proctor from Broxbourne to bring the newly-weds back down to Denham to catch a flight from Heathrow to Jersey for their honeymoon. As Broxbourne was the smallest airfield in the south, Eric was given the customary check circuit by the Chief Instructor, but when he realised we were both pilots he begged us not to argue over it! We almost had to literally tuck the tail of the aircraft into the boundary hedge to give us the longest possible take-off run. Flying up via Wolverhampton we stayed in a pub in Valley overnight, attending the wedding at noon the next day. The wedding was, of course, lovely but after the Reception I discovered that Mair had not flown before so sat in the back of the Proctor with her for the return flight, trying to put her at her ease. The visibility was hazy when we set off and became worse as we approached Birmingham. I became aware that all was not well up front – the men were surveying the landscape more frequently. Keith had wanted to do the flight planning, but had forgotten to take into account Magnetic Variation – the difference between true and magnetic north. These few degrees had angled the aircraft farther and farther away from its desired track over the ground. They were temporarily uncertain of their position – good pilots are never lost!

Nevertheless, we were running low on fuel and when we caught sight of a very large airfield thought of landing there. Suddenly we realised that it was the U.S.A.F. base of Brize Norton and that we would indeed not be at all welcome! Fortunately we recognised another landmark and were able to make it to Kidlington. After refuelling, a new course was set for Denham, checked by all three pilots, and a very relieved Keith and Mair made it to Heathrow in time, despite walking to the nearest bus stop!

....

Our next project was the acquisition of a car. It had been thought about during the Summer, but neither Eric nor I had a driving licence. My father had started teaching me to drive whilst I was still at school, but petrol rationing had put paid to his efforts. Eric had learned to drive on airfields during the War, but did not have a civil licence. It was decided that, as I had more time, I would obtain mine first.

My initial B.M.A. instructor was a highly strung ex-pilot who had been involved in an aircraft accident. He made me so nervous that I tried to use the gear lever like an aircraft stick to steer the car in the middle of the traffic in Ealing High Street! Fortunately for me he was replaced by a Police Instructor before I took my test so I managed to pass first time.

We then asked some good friends to look for a small cheap second-hand car for us. They came up with a farmer's Austin Seven 1931 Vintage for £45, which they said they would have if we didn't. However, when we went to try the car I had to back her off a narrow pathway over a wide ditch. I stalled her at least five times – the clutch movement was minute. The farmer's face said it all! I also knew nothing about double declutching, having learned to drive on a synchromesh car. Later, after frightening myself trying to change down half way up a hill, I decided to stop at the bottom next time and put her into first gear for the whole ascent. Fortunately a knowledgeable friend taught me the trick and I was then able to become more adventurous!

By this time Eric had passed the written exams for the Commercial Pilots Licence but still had a qualifying night cross-country test to do up at Stansted. He had ten bookings in all, five of which were cancelled over the phone due to weather, three for the same reason on arrival, and the 9th due a technical fault whilst taxiing out. Our little car, now named 'Georgina' (the feminine of 'George', the autopilot on an aircraft), became used to the route via the North Circular Road and stopping in

Epping Forest for hot chocolate and sandwiches!

The examiner, on Eric's 10th attempt to do his test, was 'Jock' Hunter. After briefing Eric in his office, he came into the Nissen hut, where Eric was showing me his flight plan, and sternly enquired as to who was doing the test. I waited anxiously near the fire for their return. When Eric walked in and said, with a perfectly straight face, I would have to bring him again, I couldn't believe it. Even Jock looked surprised. Unlike my father, Eric's eyes didn't give him away initially. He had in fact passed. I could have cheerfully throttled my dear husband! Jock Hunter was later to become a very close friend.

Having, at last, obtained the Commercial Licence, Eric applied to both British European Airways and BOAC only to find that he was too old at 27. He continued looking for other jobs but things were quiet over the Christmas period. In order to earn some money for presents, I found a part-time secretarial job, mainly doing book-keeping for a man who ran his own small business from home. Although I liked the family, I was glad to give it up afterwards.

I introduced a small Christmas tree to our bed-sit and bought our first Christmas Carol – it had to be Silent Night!

The start to the New Year was frustrating as it was at the bottom of the curve of the silly cycle that besets aviation – too many pilots chasing too few jobs. However, during February, Eric saw an advert in the aviation magazine 'Flight' for an instructor with a Commercial Licence at Thruxton. At the interview he was told that as well as instructing he would be required to do some Army Co-operation flying, banner towing and charter work. After ascertaining that I would be able to do some instructing as well, he accepted. The basic salary was £8 per week, but with the extras, should come up to over £10. We thought it would be a start.

A visit to the Ideal Home Exhibition convinced us that a caravan was our best bet regarding accommodation and we ordered a Berkeley 20 footer. It took nearly a month for it to be delivered from Bedford, during which time we lived in the students' quarters on the airfield. I tried to soften them a little but was glad when our new home arrived.

Work was not plentiful, however, and the banner towing contract didn't materialize. There were also some young

students becoming Assistant Instructors en route to the Commercial Licence. Eric's services were dispensed within a month after the arrival of our caravan. An Assistant Instructor was, of course, paid less than a fully qualified one!
Fate intervened once more.

Eric had become a qualified Gliding Instructor with the Air Training Corps during the War and the post of Chief Instructor at Dunstable became available that very month. We had our caravan moved back towards its base, just to the north of Dunstable. Whilst awaiting its arrival we once again lived in student quarters.

Eric had to work six days a week, and during the summer courses the hours were from 9am to 11pm as the regular members took over at the end of the day. The gliders would land by the light of car headlamps and had to be knitted into the hangar, which could take nearly an hour.

Towards the end of that summer, Eric became so exhausted that his assistant had to take over whilst he slept for a whole day and night. The enthusiastic members still couldn't understand why he didn't fly on his day off!

Prior to Dunstable I had only once been up in a glider with a friend of Eric's at Lasham. The winch launch was very exhilarating but, when the cable was released, I had nearly had heart failure – the airspeed read 40mph, the speed at which a light aircraft would fall out of the sky. No one had warned me! However, I took my courage in both hands and went solo, finally achieving the basic 'C' Certificate by flying back and forth along the hill beside Dunstable.

The advanced skilful pilots were able to attain great heights by spiralling up in Cumulus clouds and travel long distances when there were sufficient thermals (up currents). However, unlike powered aircraft pilots, they would not know exactly where they were going to land – it could be on a piece of grass anywhere. Club members, crew or family would follow them with a trailer to bring them home. Sadly there were some accidents due to pilots trying to extend their flights. On the whole I was chicken and preferred a powered aircraft, knowing that I could be independent and reasonably certain of arriving at my destination airfield.

Some glider pilots thought they were superior to those who

flew powered aircraft because they didn't use engines. They forgot that they required an engine powered winch or an aircraft tug to get them airborne in the first place! A few also thought that airliners should give way to them. However a heavily laden airliner climbing with reduced noise abatement power is not able to manoeuvre easily.

After the club acquired a Tiger Moth for towing, I helped out with the instruction of stalling and spinning. If there were insufficient thermals a glider would not be able to climb high enough to practise these exercises, and a pupil's progress could be delayed for weeks. I also ferried the Tiger backwards and forward to Denham for refuelling. If it was not required in a hurry, I would do some instructing for the Denham Club in order to build up the required hours for the renewal of my Instructors Licence.

Towards the end of the Summer the peaceful tranquillity of gliding at Dunstable was marred by the installation of a race track on the slope opposite our caravan. After seeing a nasty crash from my window, I was put off car racing for life. Undisciplined drivers and aeroplanes do not mix well on airfields, as was shown when a car blithely cut across the take-off path of the Tiger Moth, which was towing a glider. The aircraft just managed to lift off in time, pulling the glider safely up. My heart was in my mouth as I watched it happen in slow motion. I was even more angry when I learned that it was my husband in the Tiger!

We had wanted to have a family and were delighted when I started. After four months of morning sickness, becoming all day for the fourth month, I returned to flying. At that time there were no aviation rules and regulations about expectant pilots. However, spinning eventually became a bit much and when I found it awkward to get the stick back for landing, I decided enough was enough! I did one more flight with Eric in a two seater glider at the end of the day. It was a beautiful evening, but as we flew over the Lions Enclosure at Whipsnade Zoo I was overcome by an irrational fear of what would happen if we suddenly ran out of lift. All I wanted was to get the three of us safely back on the ground at Dunstable.

That was it – no more flying until our baby had arrived safely.

Chapter 9

Children And Tragedy

Early in the Spring of 1955 we fortunately learned that the Denham Flying Club needed another Instructor. Eric applied and was asked to start on the 1st May. It would only be a five and a half day week so we hoped to have a little more time together as a family. However, things are seldom simple.

Regardless of being booked into the Luton and Dunstable Hospital for the arrival of our baby around the 5th May, we had to move from Dunstable to Denham for Eric to take up his position as Instructor at the Denham Flying Club. Prior to this, 'Georgina' was involved in a small incident. Fortunately no damage was done, but it sent my blood pressure up. The hospital gave me permission to move with the caravan to Denham, provided I came back immediately. When admitted, I was put into a small room for a couple of days and allowed to sleep myself out – bliss!

A little tardy, Jon arrived at 5am on the 8th, not at all wrinkled. My first thought was that he must have been here before. Eric flew over to visit us in a Tiger from Denham that morning. The baby was, of course, known as 'the little airman'! Eric, however, had to cope with a new job, feeding himself and our cat and Scotty dog, and, due to distance, was only able to drive over every other day. At that time it was normal to stay in hospital for a week, but as Jon developed a cold we had to wait an extra few days before taking him home with great pride, but with some trepidation. En route 'Georgina' hiccupped a few times but we made it without resorting to the A.A.

According to my log-book, baby Jon's over-enthusiastic parents couldn't wait to introduce him to the air. We gave him a ten minute circuit on the 30th of that month!

Coping with a baby in a caravan was easier than I had expected. Everything was to hand. A power cable had been connected to provide electricity and there was a small integral coal fire for use in cold weather. Washing was the only slight problem.

To fill the caravan's tank, water had to be brought from a tap alongside the hangar a little distance away and the clothes and nappies (there were no disposables) would often have to be dried in the garden shed.

After six weeks of broken sleep, the District Nurse told us that some babies are not hungry in the middle of the night, only thirsty. On instructions we tried boiled water with glucose, and it worked. Soon afterwards Jon decided it wasn't worth waking up for and slept from 8pm to 8am, bless him!

On fine days I would walk him round the airfield to the Club and would sometimes be able to do an hour's instructing whilst Eric looked after him. On other occasions, friendly Club Members would be happy to care for him so that I could help out with an extra flight.

As Jon grew we bought a wooden cot and cut the legs off one end so that it fitted on top of a seat. We also bought a tin bath which, when not in use, lived in the shed. Eric's salary was approximately £12 per week so we lived very simply. On some days off we took a picnic to nearby woods and afterwards enjoyed a cider in a pub.

On other days we visited family who would offer to baby-sit so that we could go to a cinema occasionally. We wouldn't trust anyone else. Needless to say, his ever enthusiastic parents took Jon up for a special flight to celebrate his first birthday. It was, however, delayed due to a club member wanting the aircraft. As soon as the engine started he fell asleep and was oblivious to the whole shortened circuit; it was time for his mid-morning nap. He nevertheless made up for it by taking his first steps towards his father that afternoon.

During the summer Eric would often have to work late so I welcomed August when the days became noticeably shorter. At least he didn't have to knit gliders into a hangar afterwards. One summer's lunchtime, Eric looked out of the caravan window to see a Tiger Moth wallowing down to land. He rushed out thinking it would crash to find a man, who had recently obtained his Private Licence and had broken his arm, was teaching someone else to fly. It was found that Aviation Law did not stipulate that all instruction towards the Private Licence should be given by a qualified Instructor – only a certain few hours, which by no means covered the syllabus. We therefore wrote to various authorities naively expecting that the law could be changed immediately. I ended up by contacting an Opposition M.P. who I went to see at Westminster. He asked a question in the House and a new law was brought in two years later.

In the interim, we found we had another battle on our hands. Although we had permission from the owners of the airfield to position our caravan alongside that of the Chief Instructor, the farmer next door had exceeded his allowance of caravans and the Council decided to take action. We had to instruct a Barrister and appear in Court. When I had to speak I found myself saying that if anything happened to my husband, I would have to earn a living by instructing and the only way to keep my Licence valid was to live near the airfield so that I could achieve the hours needed to renew it each year. I had no idea that these words would come out. I had not previously been able to accept that I could continue without Eric; we had found too much happiness together.

Knowing that we had to show members of the Council our site, I had worked very hard on the garden and the caravan was immaculate. However, as I walked up the steps I knew something was wrong and, after they left, I lost the baby I had recently become pregnant with. We were, however, given permission to remain on the site for two years.

Basically serious, Eric could not show his emotions easily, but he was very caring. He would ask me to marry him again every 21st of the month. After the only real row we had, Eric had to go up to London. Having hung the washing on the line, I returned miserably to the caravan. Shortly afterwards there was a knock and I was asked if 'that rolling pin' was handy before a bunch of flowers was extended through the half-open door. It was probably only the second time he had given me a bouquet. Despite the adverts, I still prefer flowers to chocolates!

We were fortunate in being able to spend our September holidays in the West Country, staying with kind cousins who live in Burnham-on-Sea. With Jon we visited Kilve and he was able to play on the beaches at Weston-super-Mare and Burnham. As we still wished to give him a companion, we were delighted when I became pregnant again. This time I was only 'hors de combat' for a couple of weeks as we had heard of an air-sickness pill that helped, but by then aviation rules had changed and I was not able to continue flying.

With the hoped for increase in the family, we felt that it would be a good idea to find a job with more prospects. However Eric was more tired than I realized and did not have much energy left over for letter writing. I eventually persuaded him to advertise in 'Flight' magazine and 'The Aeroplane'. There was initially only one response which seemed at all possible but this didn't come to fruition. However, a second attempt brought other opportunities. The Cardiff Flying Club based at Pengham Moors sounded the most promising, but even then he had to apply twice as the secretary was only part-time. He would be Chief Instructor and earn a basic salary of £750 per year plus extras which could bring it up to the magical figure of £1,000! He was asked to start on the 1st of June. Our second baby was due around the 22nd May which was Nan's and Eric's birthday. The arrival would once again coincide with a move. We decided to buy another caravan, when settled, so that we wouldn't have to worry about accommodation.

Although Christopher deigned to start his arrival the night of the 22nd, he decided to have a birthday of his own. Eric tried to encourage us by flying over the Nursing Home, but Chris waited until 5am on the 24th. When he was born, he had three little furrows on his small forehead. I remember saying "Not to worry, everything was going to be alright." Eric was not allowed to visit until the evening but was thrilled with him. Unusually, when he left, my quiet, undemonstrative husband turned at the door and waved goodbye.

His Aunty Mary, who loved children, was looking after Jon while Eric packed up the caravan for the move. He was due to visit us again the next evening, but didn't arrive. I wasn't too concerned, thinking that 'Georgina' had developed a problem en route. When there was no news by the end of visiting time, I asked the Sister to phone the Flying Club, knowing that they were having a party that evening. A little later she came back and told me that he was not very well, but I mustn't worry, and gave me a sleeping pill.

Next morning I asked the nurses to phone again and was told by the Sister that my husband had been taken to hospital. I immediately said "I must go to him", but she then quietly replied "I'm afraid it's no use." Involuntarily I said "Oh no!" but knew at once that deep down I had known it would happen. He had finished all he needed to do in this life and it was his time to go on. I had to bring up the children the way he would have wanted.

Chapter 10

Preparing For A New Life

My bed was moved to a window away from the others and Christopher was brought to me. I lay there looking out at the sunshine with the future unknown. My Father and Nan decided that they must have us home and collected us at lunchtime. They had hurriedly prepared a study for us and, subsequently, organized a room for Aunty Mary and Jon.

From the moment of my arrival in my parent's home I was cocooned in the most incredible love and warmth. Until then I had not known the real love of God. Eric was also very close. We had occasionally spoken of our religious beliefs and felt that there was definitely a God. We believed that there were many different paths to Him via the various religions around the world, though sadly many were jealous of one another and some had fragmented into Sects for self-glorification.

My family were wonderfully kind and I was greatly encouraged to find that my step-mother, Nan, believed in re-incarnation. It made complete sense to me. I had previously thought that life must be like a school. One could not possibly experience everything in one life-time and therefore had to live through many in order to progress. If a life was curtailed or one did not do very well, one would return to a similar life in order to complete the necessary experience or achieve the required standard. Eric and I had both known unhappiness and insecurity during our teenage years, and through the material difficulties of our four years of marriage we had become much closer to each other than if they had been trouble free. Our love had finally given him the confidence he lacked when we first met, and the offer of the post of Chief Instructor at Pengham Moors was a culmination of his flying career. The safe arrival of his second son must have also given him a great deal of happiness.

He died of a cerebral haemorrhage whilst packing up our caravan for the move. I was only grateful it happened on the ground and not in the air. He had only recently passed his aviation medical, although there had been concern at a loss of weight which was thought might be due to tuberculosis. A second check had, however, shown him to be clear.

The funeral service was held at Golders Green. It was taken by the kind Reverend Connor who had married us at Harefield. I was also very touched when I heard about the fly past by members of the Denham Flying Club, led by the Chief Instructor 'Wilbur' Wright. My room was filled for a couple of weeks by the flowers sent by friends. They were very comforting.

I looked after my children during the next four months. My parents fortunately had a big house which they were able to sub-divide and they organized a small flatlet for us – a bedroom for the boys and a bed-sit for me with a bathroom and Baby Belling cooker in a walk-in cupboard. They also had a long enclosed garden at the back with a big lawn, tall trees and an herbaceous border. It was completely safe for Jon to play in and the baby was able to enjoy some fresh air.

Nan, who had always wanted children, almost adopted Chris when she wasn't working. She would offer to give him his early morning bottle, but was almost cured when the boiling milk put out the burning toast!

My father was involved commercially with fruit importing. When the porters went on strike at the fruit market in Covent Garden, together with other Directors he would arise at 4am to help with the unloading. Nan, trying to support him, would get up to make breakfast before he left, but it was unfortunately the time when Christopher also expected to be fed and if he didn't receive the necessary food at once, he yelled the house down! Christopher certainly made up for Jon who was so good. Christopher required sustenance overnight until he was nearly one! He had his first flight in a Heron from Croydon to Jersey when we were invited to have a short holiday with friends. Although he wouldn't remember it, it was good to be airborne again and the short break was welcome, even though I was concerned that he would disturb our friends sleep at night. I had the bottle ready and waiting!

As a Flying Instructor Eric had been an Associate Member of the British Airline Pilots Association and their solicitor kindly contacted me to offer any help that I might need. It was fortunately discovered that Eric had a policy which matured on death giving me £1,500, part of which enabled me to pay my way during the first year. I was also very grateful for a surprise gift of £50 from a London Businessmen's Society called 'The Ragamuffins'. I couldn't believe it when a very well dressed gentleman turned up on our doorstep and said that they had heard of my situation and wanted to help.

I realized however, that I would soon have to start doing something towards earning a living. My parents were not keen on my continuing to fly and did their best to dissuade me – but to no avail. After my so-called experience in the Hungaria Restaurant my stepmother did try to obtain a post for me as supervisor in charge of catering in a home for young students with in-house accommodation available. She had told me that one of your problems was that I always tried to please people, but, although appreciative of her efforts, this time I definitely said no thank you I couldn't do it.

Flying was the only thing I would be happy doing, but I only had an Assistant Instructors Rating. I needed thirty more hours to upgrade to the full rating so I initially applied to the Herts and Essex Aeroplane Club at Stapleford Tawney, and then later to the club at Elstree, and was accepted as a part-time instructor. I also felt that the only chance I had of earning a reasonable salary was to obtain the Commercial Licence. I updated Eric's postal course with Avigation and studied during the bus and tube journeys to the airfield, as well as of an evening.

I had to employ someone to look after the children during the time I was away as coping with both of them was too much for Nan's sister, Norry, who ran the household. The first Nanny had come out of retirement, but we sadly had to return her to it as she had outgrown her patience with children. The next carer remained for a few months, normally only being required twice a week. Jon fortunately had taken to his younger brother quite well, but he was, as yet, no kind of a companion. I managed to persuade a nearby nursery school to accept him at two and a half, instead of three, so that he would have other children to play with for a few hours.

I spent as much time as possible with my little family, knowing that I would not have the same opportunity when I started work full-time. Eric was very close to us and remained so for a whole year, after which I believe he had to help other people, but was nearby when needed. I later read that some wartime pilots, including Lord Dowding, at one time the Chief of Fighter Command, felt that those killed came back to help pilots still fighting, especially the inexperienced ones. This was indeed the theme of a film I had seen during the War, not just my imagination.

Having obtained the necessary hours just before Christmas, I passed the full Instructors test at Eastleigh, Southampton. I had not done many aerobatics since my Volunteer Reserve days, but managed a loop and a roll! I then concentrated on the Commercial Licence, studying well into the early hours and spent a week at Avigation's school at Ealing. My first attempt at the exams was in January 1958 when I achieved a partial pass I retook the remainder in March and, to my great relief, passed. On both occasions I was the only woman and was seated in the front row, feeling very conspicuous. I subsequently read a footnote to the first results saying I would not be allowed a retake until at least May. I had sneaked in.

As with Eric, I only now needed to pass the night cross-country so went down to Croydon to learn how. I was taught to take-off and land by night and allowed to fly locally. I had heard how easy it was to mistake the Purley Way for the flarepath and it lived up to its reputation! Cross-country flying had to be done from Fairoaks and, this time, I persuaded my early instructor, good friend and advisor, Leslie Gosling to forsake his BOAC Britannia and fly with me in a Chipmunk to Bournemouth and back. Bournemouth was easy enough to find and was very impressive with its approach lights and well lit runway, but the few goose-neck flares (paraffin lit lights in cans) at Fairoaks proved a slight problem! When setting off on my solo effort I checked the pattern of nearby lights more carefully and found it more easily on my return. Three months later, delayed by weather, I passed my test at Stansted and was awarded my Commercial Licence.

By this time I had definitely decided that I needed to start earning a full time living. Through working at Elstree I was offered the post of Chief Instructor at a club in the Midlands, but knew that I didn't have the necessary experience. I was therefore interested in the post of second instructor at Exeter. I had met the Chief Instructor, Joe Heelas, when he had helped the club at Denham for a short while.

I was invited down to Exeter for an interview on 22nd February 1958 and was accepted. After being given a standardization flight, I was put to work that very day instructing on a Tiger Moth and Auster. Joe and his wife very kindly put me up overnight and, before returning to London, I did an Army Co-operation flight with him and another hour instructing on the Auster. I was asked to do an R.A.F. Home Command Test at White Waltham in order to be able to instruct Cadets, and to start work full-time at the end of March at Exeter. I would have worked anywhere in the UK but was pleased that it would be with someone I knew and in the beautiful county of Devon.

I returned to London with my mind full of how to organize the move. This time it would be for five of us. The Nanny had recently advised me that she could not continue and I had had to advertise in the Evening News and Standard. Out of six replies only three were suitable, and only one person had turned up for an interview. This lady had separated from her husband and had a little daughter a year younger than Jon. I had not had enough time to get to know her before going down to Exeter, so had asked Aunty Mary to monitor her care of the children.

On my return, the house was very quiet. I found all the family down in the kitchen, white faced and silent. I immediately thought 'Oh God, not the children! Has anything happened to them?' There had been a fire but the children were safe. The new Nanny was someone who could not bear wool close to her skin and felt the cold. When she had put her little daughter and Jon to bed for their afternoon nap, she had switched on a little two bar heater and placed it near the window. As she closed the door, the suction pulled the light curtains over the protective grid of the heater. These started smouldering and caused Jon to cough. Thank God Aunty Mary was doing the washing up in the nearby kitchen whilst the

Nanny was putting Chris out in his pram. Jon had been told not to disturb the little girl so Aunty went in to see him and found the room filling with smoke. She rescued the children before the curtains went up in flames and the fire burned through to my sitting room. It was put out by the Fire Brigade, but the flatlet was, of course, unusable. We could never thank Aunty Mary enough. She had lived for children all her life and she had certainly saved Jon and the little girl.

Although like my parents she didn't approve of my continuing to fly she was however happy to spend as much time as possible with our small family through the ensuing years.

Chapter 11

Instructing At Exeter

My parents fortunately had a seldom used long dining room on the ground floor which we were able to use as a bedroom for the five of us. After a couple of weeks of coping awkwardly, the Nanny offered the use of her house near Newbury, whilst I looked for accommodation in the Exeter area. I accepted this provided that Aunty Mary could accompany the children. The only problem was that the Nanny used a lot of Dettol. She used it in the washing up water, the bath water and for clothes washing, apart from disinfecting the bath and toilet. Due to this excessive use of Dettol, Jon developed a rash on his ears which manifested itself in white spots on his ears when in the sun. Aunty Mary was also allergic to it and our family doctor said that its use was sadly a 'snare and delusion' – its antiseptic smell masking the fact that it was useless when added to water as a disinfectant and could be seriously harmful if used in strength or neat. She was persuaded to desist.

Joe Heelas and his wife kindly offered to put me up while I was house-hunting. After finishing work, I spent my free time looking for accommodation of any type. No one wanted two women and three children. It was suggested that if I found something for a month, I would be sure to find something more permanent to follow on. I eventually found a pretty little holiday cottage with a small shallow stream running through its garden in a valley near Ottery St. Mary and we were able to celebrate the boys birthdays there. It was available for a short period during which time I redoubled my efforts, but to no avail.

Joe came to my rescue and suggested that, as they had a rambling bungalow which was too big for them, we could move in and share it with them until my luck changed. This we did and settled in. Joe and I were able to share transport to work in the form of his motorbike. I will always remember those morning rides – fresh wind in the face.

Joe and his wife had not had much to do with children but were very tolerant. The exception came when young Jon rode his tricycle into the side of Joe's beautifully polished car. Joe was not amused!

We were kept busy during the next few months with club and cadet flying during the summer holidays. The club members seemed to accept a woman instructor without a qualm. The young cadets had no choice! A few members of the public were a little concerned when they saw a lady giving joy rides at Flying Displays – others were so fascinated they queued for another one!

I used to wonder how I would feel when I sent someone solo, but found that I was reasonably confident that, barring engine failure, he/she would return to the airfield safely. Fortunately none of my pupils, nor the aircraft, suffered a mishap.

One remembers certain pupils for what they did or what they achieved. Devon is beautiful from the air and the ground. One of the Cadets, Philip Hogge, was a born pilot and a joy to teach. On a really good day above the lovely countryside I indeed felt privileged to fly with him. He subsequently joined British Airways, becoming a Senior Captain and Chief Pilot, then Aviation Consultant in Europe, and was kind enough to write to congratulate me when I eventually became an airline pilot too.

However, another Cadet had a mania for taking off towards the nearest tall object and nearly had his scholarship revoked. Among club members there was one who would sadly never go solo due to lack of co-ordination and seemed determined to ram another aircraft refuelling at the pumps. My foot shot out onto his rudder bar and we just skimmed past. I then knew why Joe had despaired of him!

Some of the Cadets did not wish to follow a career in aviation, but it was thought that the Private Pilot's course would foster an interest which would be beneficial later on. Most of them coped well and enjoyed it. Each Cadet was only allocated a fortnight in which to complete the course. If the weather was unfavourable we would have to work overtime. This meant arriving home too late to help give the children their supper, but I was sometimes in time to bath the boys and put them to bed. After this I would often fall asleep on the adjoining bed, still clothed in my flying suit!

On days off I still tried to find some permanent accommodation. I finally realised that I didn't stand a chance of finding anything to rent and was advised to buy if at all possible. I had hoped to keep the remainder of Eric's insurance in reserve, but decided to use it as a down payment if I could find something affordable. The first step was to find a Building Society that would be prepared to lend to a woman – very few would even consider it. I found one at last. They offered me a mortgage which involved a monthly repayment equal to my week's salary of £16, over 25 years.

....

I found a house in Topsham but, after my offer was accepted, a Doctor made a higher one. I then heard of a new development taking place near the top of the little cider village of Whimple and decided to have a bungalow built. A plan had already been approved for the plot I wanted and I was able to modify it slightly. It was on a gentle ridge with a sloping back garden which was separated from a large farmer's meadow by a boundary stream hedged with bushes. At last we would have a home of our own.

It seemed that things were working out and I felt able to hire a Chipmunk to fly up to Somerset on the anniversary of Eric's death. I had scattered his ashes over the sea off Kilve on my birthday the previous year, having obtained permission from the Air Ministry. I had then hired a Chipmunk from the Airways Aero Club at Croydon and called in at Denham. The Reverend Connor had kept his ashes in the Church at Harefield and brought them to the airfield for me. It was a peaceful flight.

Sadly, things on the home front were initially not so tranquil. The lady looking after my children turned out to be a kleptomaniac and stole from Joe's wife, the purloined underwear being found under her mattress. Her estranged husband also kept phoning and she became very bad tempered, so I had to give her notice and take the children back to my long suffering parents in London. Aunty Mary once more stepped into the breach whilst I found a replacement. Through an advert in a local paper I found a homely lady who had lived on a farm. As the builder had estimated that it would take three months to build our bungalow and I had previously been happy living in a caravan, I had the bright idea that we could live on site whilst it was being built. I hired two, not knowing that someone who had been used to a big farmhouse would feel claustrophobic in them. After two days, the lady said she couldn't stand it and I had to look for something else. I found two big bed-sitting rooms in a large converted house in a nearby village and returned the caravans. To my amazement the man from whom I had hired them didn't charge me. I was indeed grateful.

We became accustomed to the new accommodation, but as our bedsits were on the first floor, the Nanny still found coping rather onerous. I learned afterwards that her recent life had been traumatic as her husband had insisted on bringing home his young girlfriend and she had slept with a pistol under her pillow. Fortunately we saw no signs of it while she was with us.

In the meanwhile, on the work front, it had been decided to give the go-ahead to a Commercial Flying Training School which Joe Heelas had proposed. After an advertising campaign, new and old pilots applied. Some service trained pilots wished to return to flying, having tired of life in other occupations, and other young pilots wanted to start a career in Civil Aviation. This type of flying, involving as it did more instrument work, kept us occupied during the more inclement weather.

There was, however, one young pupil who gave us a few headaches. Every time he returned from a flight he would have done something he shouldn't have. One could never warn him of everything before each take-off. Having not so far had any instruction in instrument flying, he was told to keep clear of clouds. On his return from Plymouth the weather deteriorated causing an increasingly low cloud base over Dartmoor. In such circumstances he had been told to come back to Exeter via the coastline.

He decided to press on, found himself in cloud and turned north instead of south. He finally shot out through a Military Danger Area, very uncertain of his position. His Guardian Angel was working overtime! He landed at a disused airfield on top of a hill and I had to go and rescue him. He was contrite, but irrepressible!

To even things out we had some very good students, among them being Mike O'Connor and John Malford Davies. They were a pleasure to teach and became good friends. John joined BEA and Mike, British United. We kept in touch for many years and Mike was, indeed, instrumental in starting me on my airline career.

With the advent of Commercial training, we had to provide night flying instruction. The syllabus required ten hours night flying including the dual and solo cross-countries. These were between Exeter and Bournemouth, and with Joe's experience, we made maps with the pattern and colours for the lights of the towns en route. We also sat on parachutes but, not having had any previous experience of using them, I had a recurring nightmare of not being able to bring my hands up from my sides to pull the rip cord. Fortunately their use was never necessary!

When night flying was laid on, we would try to do as much as possible. On one occasion, teaching 'circuits and bumps' (take off and landings), due to the late hour and lack of sleep the runway lights seemed to waver from side to side. On landing I found that one pilot just needed another hour to complete his ten, so I had a really strong cup of coffee and continued. In the meantime things once more became slightly traumatic on the home front. Needless to say, the bungalow took longer to build than anticipated and we had to spend more time than hoped in our cramped accommodation. However, we were able to move into 'Apple Blossom', the name of our new bungalow, early in the New Year. The very day we moved in my housekeeper/nanny handed in her notice! I protested that, at last, we would have the space and everything needed to make life simpler, but she was adamant. I managed to persuade her to stay until I found someone else. I think it was then that I decided that my philosophy of life was definitely 'It doesn't matter what happens to you, but how you cope with it!'

It took all of three months to find Ros, my next nanny, and I had to fly up to Bristol in an Auster to bring her down to meet us and see if she liked us. Fortunately she had been a Radar Operator in the W.A.A.F. and didn't mind this form of transport. Ros, thank goodness, decided in the affirmative and joined us with her young daughter, Janet, who was a little older than Chris. Things improved from then on. We became much more of a family unit.

I tried to help when at home, but will never know how she coped with us. We developed a custom of having a cup of coffee together in 'revival time' after putting the youngsters to bed, but Ros had to look after them all day, most days, and some evenings. We did, however, manage to pile into 'Georgina' to visit the seaside at Exmouth and Dawlish Warren, where I later taught the young to swim, Chris only condescending to learn once I had bought him his toy boat!

Ros fortunately enjoyed gardening and with the 'help' of the children we set about organizing the ground. I had planted a border of red roses in the front and had fashioned a small lawn but the sloping back was still rough grass, which we slowly tamed. We did, indeed, try transplanting a young apple tree from the next door plot at eleven o'clock one night. We were 'saving' it from being destroyed by building, but sadly it didn't survive.

I had been told, after Eric's death that it would take at least two years to feel normal again. I had, indeed, been living as a matter of duty, but almost to the day, I suddenly noticed the beauty of the trees while driving home from the airfield one calm evening, and thought God did make the world beautiful after all.

At the airport it was good working with Joe. He was a very experienced pilot. He had learned to fly before the War and, not wanting to join the family firm, had become an 'F' Reservist (later R.A.F.V.R.) through a University Air Squadron. He gained the necessary hours for a Commercial Licence by charter flying Club members from airfields in Yorkshire. Everyone was made a member to legitimise these flights! He obtained the Licence, Instrument Rating and Instructor Rating in 1936. After a few colourful jobs including legitimate charter flying, joy riding and barnstorming with a Flying Circus, he had hoped to join Imperial Airways. The Royal Air Force Volunteer Reserve, however, decided to qualify him as a Service Instructor at the Central Flying School. He was posted as Senior Instructor to Stoke-on-Trent. With the War pending, he flew an Anson full of pupils to report to R.A.F. Derby. His experience was very valuable and indeed he flew Beaufighter aircraft in the defence of Malta. I understand that he became a V.I.P. pilot and, after the War, helped the Israelis set up their flying school.

He was both philosophical and ironic, irritated by small things, but took big things in his stride. When the airport secretary ticked him off because some Cadets had not returned the books borrowed from the library on time, he took it out on

Left: Yes, this is a serious-looking Yvonne, with my father Marcel.

Below: My schoolteacher mother, Iris.

Below: My father with my step-mother Nan.

Right: as a young teenager, I was already steadfast in my desire to fly!

Part of my British Overseas Airways Corporation stewardess training included meal presentation - as laid out in chalk on a blackboard!

Right: In my Scottish Airlines stewardess uniform

Below: With BOAC Captain Leslie Gosling and his Argonaut crew.

Left: Greeted by Instructor Eric Pope on return from my first cross-country in a Miles Magister.

Right and below: Yvonne and Eric in front of the new club Auster J-5F Aiglet Trainer, little knowing that they would soon to be the first to have an engine failure in it!

ROYAL AIR FORCE VOLUNTEER RESERVE. R.A.F. Form 1048 (W)

NOTICE PAPER

_5_ years' service in the Royal Air Force Volunteer Reserve.

Signature of applicant receiving the Notice Paper ___Y. van den Hoek.___

NOTICE to be given to the applicant at the time of her offering to join the Royal Air Force Volunteer Reserve.

Date __29/9/52__ 19 .

The general conditions of the contract of enlistment that you are about to enter into with the Crown are as follows :—

1. You will engage to serve His Majesty (as a special reservist) for a period of _____ years in the Royal Air Force Volunteer Reserve, provided His Majesty should so long require your services.

2. You will be required to attend or be called out for training as explained in Question 25 of this Form.

3. You will be liable to be called out on permanent service as explained in Questions 21 and 22, and when called out on permanent service you will form part of the Regular Air Force.

4. When called out for continuous daily training or for service as explained in Questions 25, 21 and 22, you become liable to the Air Force Act ; at other times you are subject to the Reserve Forces Act, as applied to the Air Force Reserve.

5. You will be liable when called out, and if medically fit, to carry out duty in the air whenever required to do so.

6. You will not be permitted while serving in the Royal Air Force Volunteer Reserve to join any other of His Majesty's regular or non-regular forces.

7. You will be required by the Attesting Officer to answer the questions printed on pages 1, 2 and 3 of this Form, and take the oath shown on page 3, and you are hereby warned that if you wilfully or knowingly make at the time of your attestation any false answer you will thereby render yourself liable to punishment.

Signature and Rank of Officer or N.C.O. }
serving the Notice Paper }_____

ROYAL AIR FORCE VOLUNTEER RESERVE.
CERTIFIED COPY OF ATTESTATION.

No. __2672196__   Name __YVONNE ELIZABETH VAN DEN HOEK__

Questions to be put to the Recruit before enlistment into
the Royal Air Force Volunteer Reserve.

You are hereby warned that if, after enlistment, it is found that you have wilfully or knowingly made a false answer to any of the following questions you will be liable to punishment under the Air Force Act.

1. What is your name ?

2. Where were you born ?

1. Surname __VAN DEN HOEK__
   Other names __Yvonne Elizabeth__
2. In the parish of __Pretoria__ in or
   near the town of _____ in the
   county of __South Africa__

My RAF VR documentation - happily signed!

Mr and Mrs Eric Pope on our wedding day
- 21st March 1953.

My 'going away' outfit!

Above: just before flying away on honeymoon.

May 1955: Eric with our first son, Jon in front of our caravan home.

Jon's first footsteps on his birthday; 8th May 1956. This occasion went some way to make up for him falling fast asleep on his birthday flight earlier that morning!

London ⟩
To Wit ⟩

Yvonne Elizabeth Pope   was admit

into the   **Freedom**   of the Guild of Air Pilots and Air Navigat

on the **First** day of   **April 1957**

by **redemption**

            J. Lancaster Parker   Mas

                  Cl

Above: awarded to me for my contribution to air safety.

Below: Denham Aero Club's three instructors. Left to right: Eric Pope, Wilbur Wright, Chief Flying Instructor (CFI) and Joe Heelas, a highly experienced wartime pilot, who later became CFI at Exeter.

Left: Nan with baby Chris and young Jon, helping us after Eric's death.

Below: Jon, myself and Christopher on holiday in Jersey in July 1957.

Jon, Chris and Janet with Ros.

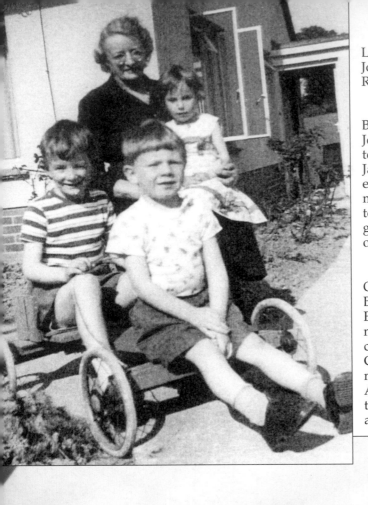

Left: Aunty Mary with Janet, Jon and Chris, Janet being Ros' daughter.

Below: Hoping to give Chris, Jon and Janet their first flight together from Exeter Airport. Janet was frightened by the engine noise and returned to mum. When airborne, Jon told me to look where I was going when I tried to point out the small houses and cars!

Opposite page: The Lennox Boyd Trophy presented to the Exeter Aero Club for being the most efficient club in the country. Left to right: Wing Commander Pearse, the managing director of Exeter Airport, me with the Cup, and two student pilots, R Wright and I A Alli.

BRITISH WOMEN PILOTS' ASSOCIATION

c/o THE WOMEN'S ENGINEERING SOCIETY,
25 FOUBERT'S PLACE, LONDON, W.1 *Telephone: GERRARD* 5212

Please reply to:- 41 Euston Road,
W. Croydon
Surrey.

14th April 1960

Mrs. Yvonne Pope,
c/o Exter Airport, Ltd.,
Honiton Clyst,
Exeter, Devon

Dear Mrs. Pope,

I am very pleased to tell you that you have been awarded the challenge cup presented by Lord Brabazon in conjunction with the Jean Lennox Bird Trophy - which as you will by now have heard has been won by Mrs. Anne Burns.

This additional cup was presented by Lord Brabazon only very recently owing to the fact that there were two distinct types of candidates nominated for the Jean Lennox Bird Trophy, (a) the woman pilot who did well on one particular flight and (b) the woman pilot who was consistent and contributed more towards aviation in general. In the latter case, the Selection Panel were unanimous in their decision to award this new trophy to you and I wonder if you could come to London on April 28th to have it presented by Lord Brabazon at the Kronfeld Club?

I do hope you can make it and would appreciate your answer as early as possible.

Our heartiest congratulations to you in winning this cup.

Yours sincerely,

Mavis Harriott

Hon. Secretary

I was very honoured to receive the Brabazon Challenge Cup.

Centre and right: my mother and sister Marcelle in my garden at Whimple, near Exeter, celebrating with the Brabazon Cup, myself, young Jon and Chris

The smallest aircraft I have flown: Dart Kitten G-AEXT

My new 'office' as seen from under the wing of a Handley Page Herald - the Air Traffic Control Tower at Stornoway.

Opposite page: accepted as an Air Traffic Controller at last!

Right: Myself with a BEA Viscount crew and controller I was replacing at Stornoway.

A somewhat bemused 'visitor' to the Control Tower at London Gatwick, a building that had not long been opened for use.

me. So I put a little note on his desk saying 'Why be awkward, when with a little effort you can be bloody impossible!' (I had read this on the wall of a Barber's shop while waiting for my son's hair to be cut!) All he did was laugh. However, when something slightly serious occurred his response was 'Don't worry, it has happened to me before.'

As the experience of our Commercial students increased, Joe felt it would be a good idea to have some information regarding the current Civil Instrument Rating requirements. This qualification was necessary to fly along airways, the civil aerial routes, and to cope with the let-downs through cloud at airports. He, of course, had all the military qualifications, but civil procedures had changed. He decided that I would benefit by obtaining this Rating. The airport manager didn't agree with him, saying that I had my work at the Club and a family to look after. I went ahead anyway.

At that time, the tests were carried out on a Dove aircraft at Stansted by the Civil Aviation Flying Examiners. My only experience of a twin engine aircraft was a short flight in a Gemini. Although this aircraft had two engines, if one failed the result was merely a slowed-down descent! By comparison the Dove was a small airliner and indeed could carry eight passengers. If an engine failed it could be safely flown on the remaining one. One had to demonstrate this following all the necessary procedures.

I had hoped that I would be able to obtain some practice on the Mosquito flown from Exeter by ex-Service pilots on Army and Navy Co-operation flights. Eric had helped in the design of the cockpits and I had looked longingly at them. However, although we were all insured by the same company, it was deemed a risk. What would happen if a tyre burst and they found a woman on board?! I then hoped I might be lucky with the R.A.F. Examiner who checked us for the renewal of our Instructors Ratings. He had been sympathetic and had said that if I could get back into uniform it might be easier. He initially had the use of his own Mosquito, but sadly lost it and was unable to use the Exeter ones to help me. I had thought that if I could cope with a Mosquito, I could cope with a Dove!

I then heard that as a member of the Royal Observer Corps, one could obtain flights in Service aircraft. So I joined, and found myself partaking in exercises plotting Atomic Fallout in an underground Headquarters near Exeter. As time was short and there weren't any Air Displays pending, I decided to go up to Chivenor in uniform on a day off. I pretended to know nothing about aircraft and asked if I could please have a flight. I was told that the Anson, which had been on maintenance, needed a check flight, but it had been delayed until the afternoon.

I was asked, 'Would you like to have lunch in the Sergeants Mess and come back later?' I happily agreed but when I returned the check had not yet taken place. I was then asked, 'Would you like to come back the next day?' I replied, 'No, unfortunately I will be working, but could I possibly see where to go the next time?'

At that moment the pilots came in and offered to take me to the other side of the airfield where I came clean. They were intrigued and took me up on the delayed check flight, when it was suddenly cleared. For the first time I misread the altimeter after we flew alongside a steep cliff – I thought it read 500ft above sea level instead of 1500 feet! The aircraft had climbed gently while I was admiring the view. I was concerned that 500ft was too low over land! Sadly the aircraft was not dual control so I was only able to stand behind and watch the use of the pitch and boost controls with which I was unfamiliar. The pilots suggested that they would fly down to Exeter to pick me up and give me some practice. Sadly this too was negated.

I couldn't afford to pay for any Dove or other twin-engine flying so went ahead with some Link (aircraft simulator) training in order to pass the required Link exam. I took a week's leave, went to stay with my parents and attended a school.

The instrument procedures required a great deal of concentration and could be rather confusing, particularly the use of the radio beacons which delineated the airway routes and were also used for airfield let downs, following set approaches to the runways. The needle of the radio compass pointed towards the beacon tuned in and showed when one passed overhead by doing a 180 degree turn. If there was a beam wind one had to angle the aircraft into it, to keep on the centre line of the airway or maintain a required track over the ground. One estimated the number of degrees to compensate for the drift and, if the anticipated angle increased when going towards the beacon, it meant that you had overdone it and were going windward away from the required track, so had to decrease the amount allowed for drift. After passing over the beacon the indications were reversed. If the angle between the heading and the radio compass needle increased, it meant that you had not allowed enough for drift!

It was important to maintain the correct track on airways as they were only ten miles wide and one was only protected from other aircraft whilst within this corridor. Attention had to be paid to speed and height. Speed had to be maintained within 5 knots as there was a longitudinal time separation between aircraft at the same height. This was adjusted according to the relative speeds of the aircraft. It could be reduced if the aircraft ahead was faster, but likewise, increased to stop the slower one being caught up. Vertical separation was 1,000ft below 29,000ft. Above this level it was 2,000ft, as altimeters were not as accurate as they are today. One had to maintain the altitude given by Air Traffic Control to within 200ft. As well as following certain specified routes when taking off from or approaching airports, it was also necessary to obey any height and speed restrictions in order to keep one clear of terrain and other traffic. It was difficult to keep the picture clear, so I learned by heart and managed to pass somehow.

I then booked the flight test. I was greatly overawed by the unfamiliar aircraft and it was all a complete nightmare. I felt so terribly inadequate and had a horrible feeling of inevitability when the door closed. Needless to say I failed miserably; it was a 'shock' experience. After my second abortive attempt, Joe Heelas decided I needed some help. He contacted someone he knew who worked for Morton Air Services and flew Doves. I was invited to sit in on an overnight paper flight from Croydon to Le Bourget which fortunately helped me to familiarize myself with the cockpit layout.

It took place just before Christmas and I will always remember the contrast in airport decoration was amazing. The terminal at Le Bourget had a Genevieve type car overflowing with gaily coloured presents beside free standing silvered branches tastefully decorated. The terminal concourse at Croydon had only a tall fir tree with paper bows.

My third attempt took place early in the New Year. This time

I managed a partial pass. The examiners and operations staff were surprisingly understanding. They realised that I was working hard at Exeter and did their best to give me advice and fit me in when it was possible for me. My fourth and fifth attempts were on the same day. Unfortunately, my alarm clock went off an hour early and I woke with a developing cold. I decided to catch an earlier train and call in at the Link School. They felt sorry for me and gave me some quinine, with the result that I was then sadly rather dazed and very happy to correct the same way both inbound and outbound during the beacon let down - instead of doing the opposite when flying away from the beacon – not only once, but twice, an attempt in the morning and another in the afternoon! When I passed on my sixth attempt I just had a feeling of sick relief. My only consolation was that it was par for the course at that time.

On the financial side, the initial cost for two plus hours flying was only £25. Halfway through the Ministry decided that we had practiced too long on their aircraft and increased the fee to £50. Through the Royal Observer Corps I had heard that the R.A.F. Benevolent Fund might be able to help me as I had been in the R.A.F.V.R. I applied and they were kind enough to offer me a £70 loan. I also wrote to the Ragamuffins who incredibly gave me another £50, although I gather that some members were not too sure that a woman should be doing this sort of thing!

As far as our Commercial students were concerned, I certainly knew what to concentrate on in their instrument flying to and from a beacon!

In the middle of my attempts at the Instrument Rating, the Ministry decided to send their examiners out to the various aviation schools which had come into being instead of doing all the basic Commercial tests at Stansted. The first examiner to come to Exeter was an ex-R.A.F.V.R. instructor whom I had known at Redhill. It was good to see him again. The next examiner was the fierce Scotsman, Captain 'Jock' Hunter. At that time we had several Pakistani pupils and, needless to say, the one who needed some extra instrument training was the last to return from a weekend in London. The weather closed in the next afternoon and no flying was possible. I saw the examiner sitting on his own in the restaurant and thought I had better accompany him. For something to say I mentioned that I was hoping to obtain the Instrument Rating. To my surprise, he invited me to have lunch with himself and his wife when I came up to Stansted. I replied that he must have a very nice wife, and he suggested that I meet her that evening as his family were staying in a nearby pub, the one we normally used. He was the examiner who had checked Eric on his Commercial Night Cross-Country test and his wife, Betty, was warm and friendly. It was the beginning of a friendship which lasted for many, many years. I did indeed have lunch with Jock and Betty in between my 4th and 5th attempts at the Rating, and on so many other occasions. Their son, Andrew, and my two boys shared some holidays when I later introduced the family to Menorca.

Earlier on, once settled in our new bungalow in Whimple, my mother came over from South Africa to visit us and see her grandchildren for the first time. My youngest sister, Marcelle, also came to see us before she went to work in Canada and America. My second sister, Toni, had already been granted a Bursary to study Deaf Teaching in both countries and has continued doing this marvellous work all her life. Aunty Mary was a more frequent visitor, wanting to keep an eye on 'her' boys. I was so fortunate to have Ros to cope on the home front. I could never have managed it all without her!

After the visits I thought it only fair that I should take my little family up for a joy ride, so booked an Auster. Unfortunately when the noisy engine started up, Ros's young daughter, Janet, took fright and they had to disembark. I put my elder son, Jon, in the front seat beside me, leaving Chris in the back. After take-off I tried to put them at their ease by mentioning how the cars and houses looked like toy ones. A very stern voice came from beside me saying "Mummy, look where you are going!" It was a short circuit!

Through being a member of the British Women Pilots Association I was awarded the Lord Brabazon of Tara Trophy for my work as an Instructor. I was very honoured and surprised and had to go up to London to receive it. Needless to say there was a mention of it in the Aero Club Newsletter which ended with 'Lord Brabazon presented his trophy for... ...to Yvonne Pope, our young, attractive and clued-up Instructor.' On one of the copies, the 'c' for clued had been rounded and a tail added in pencil to make it 'glued-up'. Underneath was written 'No comment'. Perhaps I could be pedantic and, yes, I was the 'Ice Maiden'! The comment might have been written by the Club Barman, over whom I had tipped a jug of water when he was being particularly obnoxious to someone!

In all probability we trained more than forty Commercial Pilots, but the Ministry then suddenly decided that the Ground School should be combined with the Flying School and the Exeter Airport Authorities felt that it was not worth their while. To my mind this was a pity because they had an airfield with both grass and runways, possibly adequate accommodation and enough traffic to make pupils aware of Commercial aircraft.

Shortly after this, Joe Heelas developed Glandular Fever and had to go into hospital. To my subsequent surprise, a friend of my father's wrote to him saying that the Airport Manager was quite happy to leave the running of the Club and School in my hands. However, I realized that our Commercial Training would not be able to continue and that the future was becoming uncertain.

One of the Exeter Co-operation Pilots had lost his flying licence due to a small eyesight problem, but had been able to become an Air Traffic Controller with the Ministry of Aviation. During a visit he suggested I might like to think of doing the same. I would earn more money and have security for my family. Indeed, the Ministry had just started advertising for women as well as men! I thought that there was no harm in finding out more and that, somehow, I would continue flying as well. I applied and, as I had all the qualifications required, was granted an interview. To my amazement, I was asked how I would feel about being the first woman Controller with the Ministry. I don't think I would have accepted had I known what I was in for!

After my last afternoon's instructing, I achieved that flight in an Exeter Co-operation aircraft. Not a Mosquito, but a two-seat Vampire T-11. One of the pilots, who was also leaving, invited me to join him on a Salisbury Plain detail. It was my first flight in a jet and the low –level mock attacks on Army positions were fantastic – and we didn't burst a tyre on landing!

Chapter 12

Air Traffic Control

I reported to the Air Traffic Control School at Hurn Airport, Bournemouth on a damp September morning – and then began one of the least enjoyable periods of my life.

During our introductory lecture we were told that the purpose of Air Traffic Control was to provide a safe, orderly and expeditious flow of air traffic and that if we ever found ourselves in a Court of Law, we must be certain that we had obeyed all the laid-down procedures to the letter and could not be blamed. I was disappointed that they did not say that we were there to help the pilots all we could.

We were told that there was a list of Hotel/Boarding House accommodation available in the area. I chose a Guest House at random and settled into my small room with a one bar electric fire and a view of roofs and a long street. So began an era of periodic hotel life.

Early on in the course we were taught the eleven duties of Tower Controller and the thirteen duties of an Approach Controller. These had to be learnt off by heart and then repeated for tests. We were also introduced to the different types of Controlled Airspace and our responsibilities for the safe separation of aircraft therein. Pilots of course had to be able to use radio to fly within them.

Each busy airport had its own Control Zone which extended from ground level usually up to 2,000 feet and varied in shape and dimension. Curiously the Bournemouth zone was larger than the Gatwick one.

Terminal Areas surrounded the zones and were from a pre-determined height upwards, in order to afford some protection to the aircraft climbing up to and descending from airways, as well as those flying between airports in a congested area such as London. The airways were the arterial roads which spanned the country and within which aircraft were separated by height and speed. If outside the zones, uncontrolled aircraft were able to fly under the Terminal Areas and airways without reporting to Air Traffic Control. It was a help if they had a radio and could report their positions and intentions, as I later found out when I became a Radar Controller.

Away from the controlled network the sky was divided into Flight Information Regions within which were Advisory Routes. Assistance could be given to radio-equipped aircraft by providing them with details of other known aircraft. Non-radio aircraft had to maintain their own separation visually or, if in cloud, above 3,000 feet at certain advised heights according to heading. This gave a minimum of 500ft for crossing traffic and hopefully for head on – 1,000ft. Fortunately not many private pilots flew in cloud!

Although I had the qualifications of a Commercial Pilot and had been accepted as a Flying Instructor, many of the men on the course felt I was usurping a man's place. They thought I just wanted to become a Controller to prove that a woman could do it. They did not realise that I too had a family to support. I think it was 95% against and I was initially ostracised by most of them and pointed remarks were made when I entered the room. It was a bit of a shock and each weekend home was a welcome respite from the chauvinistic atmosphere I was experiencing.

The course continued with the method of recording and displaying aircraft details on the board in front of the controller. There were different coloured thin cardboard strips for easy identification – blue for outbound, beige for inbound and pink for local flights. These slips were slotted into metal holders and placed in the control board racks. Four letter codes were used for aerodromes, i.e. EGLL for London Heathrow and EGKK for London Gatwick. Other codes were used for aircraft types.

In the airport briefing rooms, aerodrome information was also initially supplied in code form, later to be written out in plain language by the assistants. I will always remember one code indication 'Runway marked by trees'! I didn't believe it but later, when I flew to Stockholm one winter, I found that the runway was indeed marked by small soft fir trees sticking through the snow. I still have nightmares about finding my aircraft in the middle of an avenue of trees!

The basics of navigation, radar and meteorology were also

included, all of which were important to a controller as well as a pilot. Sadly the attitude of most of the men, including one or two instructors, remained unwelcoming. Studying alone in my bedroom one night, I wept out of sheer frustration. However, it just made me all the more determined to show them that I could do it. Weekends at home kept me going, but on my return to Hurn one Sunday night, I must admit that I was filled with such black hatred that I found myself a quarter of an hour along the road to London before a road sign caught my attention and I had to backtrack to the fork for Bournemouth. That really shook me and I decided that this was not the way to cope. I had burnt my boats and knew I had to continue whether I liked it or not. Fortunately there was another pilot on the course, as well as a very experienced ex-International Aeradio Controller, who encouraged me. Their kindness helped enormously. We made a threesome for lunch.

Things also improved when we went on to the practical training. We started working with control board mock-ups, simulating Approach and Tower control. We two pilots were teamed together and took it in turns to be pilot and controller. After overcoming our initial embarrassment, we occasionally had some fun – it was better than being in the classroom! On the serious side, we practised how to cope with emergencies such as aircraft with engine failures, fires, propeller overspeeds, undercarriage failures and bomb scares. One had to alert, or call in, various numbers of fire engines and ambulances according to the severity of the problem and the number of souls on board. On take-off and landing, aircraft were limited by windspeed and direction, especially crosswinds which could blow them off the runway. If conditions were marginal it was necessary to position a fire engine near the runway in use.

During this period the person who had previously been the Air Traffic Control Officer in charge, A.T.C.O. i/c, returned to Hurn. He had been transferred to Southampton when it had been taken over by the Ministry. However, when it reverted to the Local Authority, he was posted back to Hurn as Training Officer. I understand that whilst A.T.C.O. i/c he had not even wanted any women assistants in his Tower. He was definitely not best pleased to be confronted with the first woman controller in training. He did everything he could to dissuade me from continuing, even suggesting that I should join the C.A.F.U., the Ministry's Examining Unit for Pilots! This being a complete impossibility and way beyond my wildest dreams, I had to stay put.

In between simulation work and later Tower duties, we were able to act as 'Safety Pilots' for the Ministry Pilots, who flew as Radar Targets for trainee controllers, enabling them to practice positioning aircraft around the aerodrome and in to land on the runway. Whilst the pilot concentrated on instrument flying, we checked for other traffic. After initially flying the courses given, the pilot had to pretend to be inexperienced and would deliberately fly left or right, high or low so that the trainee would have to give corrective instructions. It was great to be airborne again and I was often allowed to do the flying.

To my amazement, one of the Ministry pilots, known to me from my efforts at the Instrument Rating, suggested that I should help them officially with the flying and, indeed, introduced me to the Fleet Commander, Captain 'Jock' Keir, who also happened to be there. He happily gave his approval, but Air Traffic did not! They said permission could only be given once I had qualified as a controller. Nevertheless, the thought had helped my sagging morale.

However, another idea came to fruition. One of the Ministry's navigators, Ian Selwyn, wished to become an Examiner, but had to have an Instructor's Rating. As a pilot he already flew the Dove, assisting with target flying as well as navigating the Pembroke during the calibration of airport radio beacons and let-down systems. I had given some Instructors Courses at Exeter and the Commander, incredibly, authorized my doing so for Ian. We were able to organize this during time off.

After graduating to the Tower, life became more interesting. The controllers were pleasant and helpful and soon let us get on with it, whilst they enjoyed a cup of tea. The traffic was mixed – airline, charter and executive aircraft as well as Vampire jets co-operating with the Navy and light aircraft. Jersey Airlines was one of our regulars and some of the Captains would come up for a chat. On one occasion, Bill Maybey was delighted to tell us that instead of returning to the Channel Islands, he was going on up to Leeds. After take-off, he turned south as usual and then the R.T. was definitely less than formal: 'Hey Bill, aren't you supposed to be going north today?!' Likewise Ian Selwyn had the pleasant habit of saying 'Thank you kindly Sir/Madam' when given a clearance. I adopted it when the pilots did as requested, but inevitably on one occasion the reply came back.

'I'm not really – I'm a brute!'

Although the Controllers were satisfied with us, when it came to the practical exam, just before Christmas, only myself and the other pilot were failed by the Training Officer and the Examiner. It seemed that pilots were not very popular!

I had been informed that it was likely that I would be posted to Gatwick or Heathrow as my second training station and thought that, as Exeter was closer to Bournemouth than London, I would bide my time and do the extra month required before being re-examined. The other pilot's home was Stansted, which was also a training station. However, he had been informed that he would be posted to Lands End, despite the fact that we had been told that we could request our preferred second station. Hurn was therefore also closer to home for both of us.

When we were failed again at the end of the extra month, I saw red and demanded to see the Air Traffic Control Officer Chief in London. As I went up the steps of the building I met my friend coming out and asked him how he had fared. He told me he had been posted to Manchester! This made me even more angry. When I was shown in I was told that I had done reasonably well in the classroom, but seemed very nervous in the Tower. I responded that I had, unfortunately, inherited a shaky hand from my father. I had had a very busy summer instructing and, when I was tired, it trembled slightly. It did not mean that I was nervous and, in fact, I was prepared to work in any Tower in the U.K., in front of anyone he chose. I don't think he had ever been spoken to like that. He stuttered: 'W-we have thought of posting you to Gatwick, b-but what about your family?'

'I have everything under control', I replied.

'W-when would you like to start?' he asked.

'Tomorrow' was my reply.

I was asked to take a seat outside his office whilst he made a phone call. He came back and said I could start the next week! Fortunately the A.T.C.O. i/c at Gatwick was a reasonable man and had several women assistants. It didn't matter what sex or colour you were as long as you could do the job. The Controllers were pleasant and the women very helpful. We had a four watch system, working 1pm - 8pm with the night off, 8am - 1pm with the afternoon off, then 8pm – 8am. The rest of the day was a sleeping day, which was followed by a day off. Then one started all over again. The traffic was mainly airline – British United, Morton Air Service and Dan-Air being based at Gatwick. It was also used by executive aircraft and some light ones equipped with radio.

The Tower at Gatwick, however, did not have a Staff Rest Room, as did the one at Heathrow. I was told it was because the population of the nearest town, Horley, was less than that of Hounslow, the closest town to Heathrow. As Gatwick had not yet become busy overnight, the latter part of the night watch was divided into two sections. After supper at approximately 11pm, in a small kitchen, one half of the watch would bed down on stretchers in the nearby offices until 3am. They would then take over from the other half until 8am and vice versa. I would opt to work first half, if possible, so that I would be free to leave at 3am and return to Exeter in time for breakfast with the children. However, when I found myself on the wrong side of the road half way home, I decided a few hours sleep at my parents' home in Hindhead would be wiser.

I obtained the Aerodrome Rating at Gatwick without any trouble and then found that Stansted was to be my 'second' station.

....

Stansted to Exeter was, however, just too far. It was re-affirmed that I would be finally posted to Heathrow or Gatwick so I put my bungalow in Whimple on the market. My father and Nan suggested that somewhere near them would be equidistant from both airports. It would also mean that they could help Ros with the children. Indeed, Nan found us a bungalow with a school nearby in Grayshott.

I found a buyer for my Whimple bungalow quite quickly, but the purchase of his house was delayed by six months and I had to take out a loan for the deposit on our new home. I had joined Air Traffic to improve finances for my family and, ironically, found myself in debt for the first time in my life, to the tune of £1,000! Fortunately my initial salary of £1,100 had risen to be in line with the men's, i.e. £1,500 per annum which helped me pay the required instalments. Incredibly, I was able to repay the loan completely within a year. Eric's mother once more came to the rescue. It is wonderful how help comes from the most unexpected sources. She had previously helped me when I most needed it, giving me £500 after selling a small property. My poor car, 'Georgina', had finally started failing after many stalwart journeys from Exeter to London and back and the cheque had arrived out of the blue a week after Joe had insisted I buy another one. He was able to help me find a second-hand Austin A30 which I reluctantly thanked when I reached London without a breakdown. A young student bought 'Georgina' for £17.10s and I hope cosseted her as she deserved.

Very sadly, Eric's mother suffered with Multiple Sclerosis for several years. When she could not longer cope on her own in Ealing, I had had a bungalow built for her next to mine in Whimple so that we could help her. Unfortunately, after only six months, her condition deteriorated to the extent that she needed the full-time care of a Nursing Home. After our move to Grayshott she was transferred to a nearby hospital to that we could visit her frequently. When her bungalow was sold, her gift to me was £1,000. This enabled me to repay the loan and start again with a clean slate. I still marvel at the fantastic help I received from her.

I was not best pleased at being posted to Stansted as it brought back memories of having to pass flying tests. However, I received more help there in a most unexpected way and it proved to be another stepping stone. On reporting to the Tower I was given a very courteous note from the A.T.C. Officer i/c, Mr Stanley, apologising for not being there to greet me, and it was he who later suggested to the Air Traffic Authorities that there was no reason why I shouldn't be checked out on the Dove during my time off! I couldn't believe it and was thrilled to be allowed to fly the Dove, although still very much in awe of it.

Stansted was very much more of a training airfield than Gatwick, for airlines as well as would-be Commercial pilots, so I also managed a super-numerary flight in a BEA Vanguard. It seemed enormous. At the other end of the scale I was able to continue the Instructor's Course with Ian Selwyn on the Ministry's Chipmunks. He had previously had to fly a friend's Auster down to Redhill near Gatwick. Initially he wasn't very keen on the spinning exercise, but when he got the hang of it he didn't want to stop! I had to beg for mercy. In return he gave me some valuable tips on instrument flying.

Ian had become a flying enthusiast at the age of sixteen after a flight with Sir Alan Cobham's Flying Circus. In order to become a pilot, he had joined the R.A.F. at seventeen, but due to unforeseen circumstances, had had to retrain as a navigator. He flew as such on Ansons and Halifaxes, ending the War with Tactical Air Command which specialized in towing gliders and dropping parachutists. On leaving the R.A.F. he had joined a civil Charter Company flying as navigator and wireless operator and had then been accepted by the Civil Aviation Flying Unit as a navigator, obtaining his pilot's licence en route. After qualifying as an instructor, Ian went on to become the Staff Pilot for the Government in Kenya, where he was responsible for all the examining, calibration of radio aids and surveying in the country. A few years later he and his wife, Norah, very kindly put me up in Nairobi and helped me on my way to visit my mother in South Africa. Having been educated at Christ's Hospital in Horsham, it was he who suggested that I could send my sons to the 'Blue Coat' or one of the associated schools.

However, whilst I was at Stansted it was the incredible kindness of Jock and Betty Hunter which made my life bearable. Although I had a room in a pub in a nearby village, it was very solitary. Their home in the village of Stansted itself became my 'second home'. To share in a warm family atmosphere made all the difference. It was particularly appreciated after my car became the 'jam in the sandwich' one evening when driving through Watford on my way home to Grayshott for the weekend. The car two ahead of me failed to signal prior to turning right and the car in front of me had to brake suddenly. The road was wet and greasy and, although I braked hard, my car just touched his bumper. But the car behind me was going too fast to stop and shunted me forward very forcefully, damaging my radiator and boot. The repairs took several weeks, during which time I had to take bus, train, tube, train and bus. However, Jock or Betty would meet me on my return and take me home for the night.

I always felt somewhat uneasy about working at Stansted as there was, at that time, insufficient controlled airspace in the vicinity to protect the aircraft. The adjacent airfield, Weathersfield, used by the U.S.A.A.F. also made the situation more complex.

Although very grateful for the kindness received and for the opportunity to be checked out on the Dove, I was very relieved when I was assessed as having passed my 'second airfield' and was posted back to Gatwick. I became a fully qualified Air Traffic Control Officer Grade III (unestablished) on the 31st October 1960. I had to be checked out again on the procedures at Gatwick, but was at last able to spend more time with my family.

....

Life then settled into a more normal routine, but I eventually found that the hour long journeys to and from the airport on a regular basis became somewhat tiring, particularly the three required for the morning and night watches. I decided to move nearer to Gatwick and found a bungalow in Horsham within easy walking distance of schools. We were happier there, as the one at Grayshott had an uneasy atmosphere and noises could be heard at night. We afterwards learned that a suspected murder was supposed to have been committed there!

At work I found that the female voice was sometimes an advantage. Gatwick and Heathrow shared the same frequency for their Fire Services. On occasions, due to a certain meteorological phenomena, a condition would occur whereby a conversation could be heard over unusual distances. One day, one of our fire vehicles asked for permission to cross our runway. As it was clear, this was given. However my permission was heard at Heathrow by the same numbered vehicle waiting to cross one of their active runways.

Hearing a woman's voice, he did a double take and checked with his Tower. The Heathrow fire frequency was swiftly changed! However, to counteract this, an inbound French private pilot, on hearing a woman's voice, decided that this could not possibly be Gatwick and diverted to Biggin Hill!

Most of the pilots were used to saying 'Thank you Sir' and 'Good day Sir' but came round to 'Ma'am' quite quickly. However, habit dies hard and shortly after my return, having cleared a departing aircraft to the next frequency, I was called 'Sir' but quickly had a phone call from his company, saying 'the Captain sends his apologies – he does know the difference!' During the War the pilots had greatly appreciated the voice of a woman Controller and I later heard from the Dan-Air crews that it also revived them at 6am after a long overnight flight.

As a fully qualified Controller, I was now allowed to help with Radar Target Flying and occasionally went down to Bournemouth on days off, but also did some flying for newly qualified Precision Let Down Controllers at Gatwick who needed experience to bring aircraft safely down onto their home runway.

After working on Tower and Approach duties for over a year, I began to long to do more flying. About that time, an ex-pupil of mine, Mike O'Connor, who had joined British United Airways, was transferred with Dakotas to their associate company, Mortons. Taxiing past the Tower one morning he suggested a flight. I couldn't refuse and shortly afterwards found myself doing a night paper flight to Guernsey.

The Captain happened to be the Company's training Captain, Charles Argles, who allowed me to sit in his seat once we were airborne, with my ex-pupil, to teach me something about the Dakota. At Guernsey, the Controller kindly gave us tea in the Tower and on our way down to the tarmac, Captain Argles asked if I would like to fly the aircraft back. He started it up and taxied it past a Viscount and then talked me through the take-off and climb, giving me all the necessary speeds and settings. Having flown the Dove, I was able to cope reasonably well, despite a high approach from 3,000 feet over Dunsfold. I was then invited to fly with them whenever I had the spare time. I was delighted as it would give me some route experience; I only flew the Dove around Stansted, Gatwick and Bournemouth.

I happily went on a few of the night paper flights to Hanover, Dusseldorf and the Channel Islands and was often allowed to fly the aircraft if there were no payloads on the return journey. On occasions this included the Heron, used on the Channel Island routes. Little did I realise that this was the first step on the rung of airline flying, nor that I would eventually do some 2,500 hours on Dakotas and a few hundred on Herons.

....

Air Traffic, however, interrupted my flying by sending me to Stornoway in the Hebrides for three months. This was Gatwick's out-station, which was manned in turn by one of our Controllers, and my turn came at the beginning of 1963. I had to fly up there on New Year's Eve.

Unfortunately, Ros had developed a health problem and felt it best to accept her cousin's invitation to live in Coventry and do a more sedentary job. I was very sorry to lose her as I felt we had been a real little family unit and she had brought much happiness and continuity into our lives. However, I quite understood and we have remained really good friends. As my sons had had so many carers in their young lives, I decided to take advantage of my parent's suggestion to send the boys to a weekly boarding school in Haslemere where they would be able to have them at weekends whilst I was away. Aunty Mary wanted to have the boys with her over New Year and until the term began so I drove them up to her home the afternoon of the 30th December. It had been snowing for a while and on my return to Horsham to complete the packing up, I found part of the road was reduced to one lane through a deep snow drift. I returned to London via another route!

I had wanted to let my bungalow for the three months I would be away but found it was too short a time for anyone to be interested. However, I was told that it was usual to go on a three months Radar Course on returning from Stornoway, so I followed the advice of a friend and let it to the Army. Their minimum time was six months but they would indeed be responsible for its condition at the end of the period.

Three different lots of packing were therefore necessary: the clothes and toys for the children, my own clothes and the putting away of personal items in the bungalow, as well as leaving it clean and tidy. I hadn't managed to do it all in time to make only the one journey. I reached Harmondsworth at 10pm as our good friends, Keith & Mair, had offered to put me up overnight. We were up at 5am for Keith to take me to the airport for the early morning flight to Glasgow.

I was on the last flight to leave Heathrow before it was closed due to the rutted snow. As the Vanguard lumbered into the air I thought of my young sons and prayed that they would be kept safe. Some people had said that as a widow with young children I should not have to go up to Stornoway, but as the first woman Controller, I could not ask for any exceptions. I had been told that a woman must not bring her family into work, even though men could do so.

As we flew northwards the snow decreased and when we landed at Glasgow it was less than two inches. We were late in taking off from Heathrow so the Viscount had had to wait. It couldn't go without the new Controller, but the crew were not best pleased! En route I apologised and spent the rest of the flight, via Benbecula, to Stornoway in the cockpit. I was fascinated when shown the beach on the Island of Barra where aircraft were able to land.

Due to the Gulfstream that flows around the Islands there was very little snow at Stornoway. Immediately after landing I went up to the Tower to greet the Controller. Shortly afterwards someone came in with half a bottle of Whisky in one pocket and three glasses in the other. The Viscount was the last flight of the day and once it was airborne and well on its way we toasted the coming New Year!

The normal handover took three days, but as New Year's Day was a public holiday in Scotland, my colleague thought he had better start doing so as soon as possible and began briefing me at once. He had had to spend Christmas away from his family and was longing to return for a late celebration. The airfield closed at 5pm and he then drove me to our 'digs' where I was greeted by our pleasant hosts, Mr and Mrs Macleod. After a hot supper we repaired to the main Hotel, had a couple of drinks – whisky of course – and then went on to a dance. The spectators were treated to the spectacle of the two Controllers attempting the Scottish Reel! To my surprise the dance ended at 11pm and we then started the typical rounds of houses, seeing the New Year in at one and then going onto a series of others with eight of us in a small car, three in front and five in the back! At each home a warm welcome and wonderful array of food awaited us and it seemed that every family boasted a gold medallist in music – piano, violin and/or voice. Apart from being away from my own family, it was the best New Year celebration I have ever had. We faded out at 5am and were very grateful that New Year's Day was indeed a holiday! We had stuck to whisky and must have imbibed three-quarters of a bottle each, but had no hangover having eaten an elegant sufficiency in between.

As was her custom on Sundays, Mrs Macleod brought us breakfast in bed at 10am and we were allowed to surface slowly. There was normally no heating in the house other than an open fire in the sitting room, which was only lit late afternoon and kept in over Saturday nights. However, as I was their only lady guest, they kindly brought down an old electric fire from the attic and plugged it into the socket in my bedroom.

It went bang – and that was the end of that! I had to make do with a hot water bottle and flannelette sheets! Being a cold soul, I ended up wearing two of most things and sometimes three. I would also wear gloves and a scarf when writing letters to my boys in bed on a Sunday morning.

After a couple of days the snow turned icy which made it a little tricky when descending the hill into the centre of Stornoway to pick up the airport staff. One never knew whether the Bedford van would stop at the intersections of crossing roads on the way down. We always preceded the sanding lorry out to the aerodrome and I had to put the nearside wheels on the grass verge of the entry incline to obtain some purchase. I had never driven anything other than my own humble car and was nervous of trying any other type, even when offered. At Stornoway I found myself driving three different varieties.

The Tower, at least, was kept reasonably warm due to the equipment it housed. One of my first duties of the day was to check the weather forecast. I was more worried about conditions down South than in our area. Although the temperatures dropped some degrees below zero at night, we had nothing like the big freeze of 1963 that was suffered in England. In fact the conditions there were so bad that the start of the boys' term was delayed due to the school's boiler bursting and my parents were indeed unable to collect them from London for some days.

I had been warned about having to bend double in the 100 mph gales in the Hebrides but we had none of these during my stay. In fact the weather was incredibly calm and clear, which was just as well as the main runway was being resurfaced for N.A.T.O aircraft and Service lighting being installed alongside the Civil. Until then I had not realized that Service lights were omni-directional whereas the Civil bi-directional lights could only be seen from certain angles and on the approach. I was later to wish that Gatwick also had Service lighting.

My abiding memory of the airfield will always be picking up stones from the runway in use. This was used by the lorries transporting gravel to the N.A.T.O. one and there were inevitably some spills. I had to check it after the Fire Service had swept it and would have to pick up the vagrant pieces. The Viscounts indeed had their tyre pressures lowered so that any unseen grit would not cause a puncture.

A hand-held Aldis signal lamp was used to control vehicles wishing to enter or cross the threshold of the runway and I was loaned someone from the construction company to operate it. Although our main traffic was the scheduled Viscount, any other aircraft flight planned to arrive at least half an hour before or after it, always seemed to turn up at the same time. An Air Force aircraft did just that and followed the Viscount swiftly in. The waiting vehicle could not believe that the red light was being held on and inched towards the runway threshold, only to have a Beverley swish past its nose!

Many of the Viscount pilots were Manchester based and were standing in for those from Renfrew, who were on a course. As the regulars returned, the RT reverted to being much more light-hearted, unusual calls being used to signify crossing the coast, base leg and finals. Prior to the N.A.T.O. renovation, sheep were allowed to graze on the grass near the runways. A stray sheepdog suddenly appeared one afternoon, running down the slope towards the runway in use when the Viscount was on short finals.

I warned the aircraft I would be firing a Very cartridge. The reply was 'You brute, you!' At least the dog understood and veered away, which is more than I can say for the workman who, on one occasion, continued to cross the runway, despite the warning when I returned to Gatwick.

There were no assistants or briefing officers at Stornaway, only the Controller who had to do everything. I didn't much enjoy keeping the necessary information up to date, but it passed the time in between our few movements. One thing I did appreciate was being able to contact Scottish Division direct to talk over any problems and get them sorted out then and there.

To occupy the evening I knitted pullovers for the boys. We did, of course, watch TV and were sometimes joined by the next-door neighbour when he had to make or answer a phone call. He enjoyed football and boxing, but disapproved of us watching television on Sundays! I tried Scottish Dancing but my hip didn't take kindly to it so sadly had to desist. I did, however, enjoy the haunting beauty of Gaelic folk songs and bought some records which I have appreciated over the years.

Towards the end of my stay a friend, who worked for BEA came up for a few days and the Met Officer kindly offered her car for us to explore the Island. We drove to the other side and were intrigued by the collection of peat and entranced by the muted colours of the hills and heather. The cliffs on the western coast had a wild beauty. I thought I would like to return with my sons but unfortunately never managed it. After my return to Gatwick I did at least receive a letter from Scottish Division saying that I had not let the side down and that this would be noted in my personnel file.

Although I had been able to phone the boys over the weekends, I had longed to see them again and had counted the days. It had been planned to return to Devon for the Easter holiday to stay with a good friend in Whimple. However, just before the end of term, they both caught Mumps and this was followed by Chickenpox! We were unable to spend the holiday with my parents as my father's health was not very good and he had not had Chickenpox when young. They were afraid of his catching Shingles. Fortunately, friends of theirs kindly came to the rescue and offered the use of their gate house, which was cordoned off with rope to make a quarantine area to protect their children. That holiday was spent in keeping the coal fires going in the rooms and in keeping the children occupied. They recovered in time for the start of the new term and I returned to Gatwick. Unfortunately the Radar Course did not follow on.

During my first week back in the Tower, I couldn't believe it when a workman, taking a short cut home, walked straight towards the runway and took no notice of my red Very flare. Fortunately the inbound jet was just far enough out for him to achieve his goal! At least the birds took notice when I had to fire a Very before President Kennedy's Air Force One could take off – though I believe it nearly gave the watching Security and Press a heart attack!

We also had a problem with a taxiway from the new hangars the other side of the runway. If an aircraft came beyond a bend when approaching the normal holding point for a westerly take-off it would interfere with the Instrument Landing System, I.L.S., causing the signals to be erroneous for the incoming pilots. We therefore had to advise them to 'hold at the bend'. This took up RT time and could be forgotten if busy with other aircraft taking off and landing, vehicles manoeuvring and phone calls. At that time Gatwick did not have a separate Ground Controller so the Tower was responsible for four different frequencies at the same time – ground, air, fire and vehicle! All that was necessary was the required white line being painted on the bend and an appropriate sign to be erected. Despite several memos, nothing happened until one day, to our surprise, the Control van found a really solid wooden sign at the bend, but no white line. As aerodrome signs are supposed to be frangible, so that if touched with a wing tip no damage would be done, I ordered it to be removed immediately! Tired of waiting, another Controller and I decided to paint a white line ourselves during our next night duty. Although the Control van actually found a pot of white paint on the airfield that morning, unfortunately, it rained that night! Summoned to the A.T.C.O. i/c's office the next day, he exploded with 'What's this I hear about your wanting to paint lines on my airfield?!' The line was, however, painted the following day and a frangible sign erected!

I was also not very popular over airfield lighting. Gatwick was Heathrow's number one diversion and vice-versa. Fog density could vary at the two airports. However, Gatwick did not have the same taxiway lighting as Heathrow, where green centre-line lighting could be selected section by section to guide the pilots. It still had some of the old R.A.F. small blue lights either side of the intersecting junctions, which were not easy to see in reduced visibility without guiding green lights. Unfortunately the block of centre-line lighting, if switched selectively on the main taxiway, would stop between the two intersections, with the next section leading on to the northern taxiway.

If the apron was full of diverted aircraft, and the pilot also missed the second intersection, he would be guided towards aircraft parked on that taxiway. The aircraft could not turn round and would have to be towed backwards. Unlike Heathrow, we did not have Ground Radar and could only warn the pilot to look out for those blue lights.

Shortly after complaining about the situation, a Lighting Inspector happened to come down from London. Whilst on duty in the Tower I mentioned my concern rather forcefully. His comment to the Supervisor behind me was 'I'm glad I'm not her husband!'

It took time for anything to be done, but in the meanwhile, when on duty in fog, I decided to minimise the risk by asking the electricians to remove the offending bulbs beyond the first intersection.

....

Until I could move back into my own home I was, of course, a nomad and had to rely on family and kind friends for a bed. Shifts permitting, I saw my boys over weekends. Mid-week I took the opportunity to do some continuity flying on the Dove and build up my night hours. After a night duty, I would grab a couple of hours sleep at the nearby home of a motherly assistant and then drive up to Stansted to stay a couple of nights with Jock and Betty Hunter. They would let me sleep on arrival and whilst Jock aided and abetted me, Betty sustained me. They could not have been kinder.

Having started as an Apprentice Navigator with the Merchant Navy, Jock had changed course and joined the R.A.F. before the War, during which he flew Blenheims and was shot down over the North African desert. After walking for three days he was rescued by Arabs. During those three days he knew he had been accompanied by a Higher Power. He went on to fly Mosquitos and became a Pathfinder and V.I.P. Pilot. After the War he became an Examiner with the Civil Aviation Flying Unit at Gatwick and then moved with it to Stansted. He became my mentor, advisor and really good friend, as did Betty. I was also very kindly invited to stay with Mike and Mary O'Connor near Gatwick and was able to do some more paper flights with Mike before being posed on my Approach Radar Course – just after I had moved back home!

Approach Surveillance Radar was used to position aircraft around the aerodrome and onto the final approach for the runway in use. It could be used for normal approach in cloud down to two miles from touchdown, or when necessary, emergency positioning for a short landing. Precision Approach Radar, P.A.R., could be used to bring an aircraft on a normal straight in approach right down onto the runway, like an R.A.F. talk-down, but was normally only used down to 200 feet from touchdown. It comprised two different displays, one indicating the final heading and the other the correct glide path. This was more advanced and required a separate course.

At first I was completely mystified as to how anyone could identify the tiny dots on the screen, but gradually became accustomed to their size. At that time there was no secondary radar to give height and identification. Whilst on the course, Jock came down to Hurn to do some radio aid calibration and stayed in the same guest house. With déjà-vu he decided that I needed to know something about 'Performance A'. One had to work out a safe take-off weight for a stated passenger aircraft so that, in the event of an engine failure on or just after take-off, the aircraft could clear obstacles on the flight path and climb safely away. Careful slide rule computations had to be transferred to a graph. After supper was cleared away and washed up, he would escort me down to the kitchen where he would explain the intricacies of 'Performance A'. He was a good teacher, patient, but firm. I was not allowed to admit defeat and it certainly helped when I eventually took the Airline Transport Pilots exams.

I was, however, ticked off in my final Radar exam for saying 'Thank you' instead of 'Roger' in response to information given by a pilot. I pointed out that they both took up the same time on the RT and that I had found 'Thank you' helped a lot more. A little courtesy went a long way towards good relations between pilot and controller!

Working on radar back at Gatwick, I found that the situation was much more complex than I had previously realised. The aircraft were not as safe as I had imagined. We had two different types of ex-Service radar, one screen being positioned above the other. When directing or monitoring an inbound aircraft from our holding beacon, Mayfield, onto final approach it could disappear when at a tangential angle to the head of one of the radars and the Controller had to quickly look for it on the other screen. That one, however, had a problem with fade out at certain speeds. Added to this was the fact that the lowest level at Mayfield also faded in and out of radar coverage and unknown aircraft could be passing through the area of the holding aircraft at the same level. Mayfield was outside the zone in which aircraft had to communicate with us. As the zone only extended up to 2,000 feet anyone could fly outside it and over it at 2,100 feet without talking to us. This is the height at which an inbound aircraft would be at seven miles out if following the I.L.S. On one occasion I had to turn an inbound passenger airliner away from a sudden blip which appeared on the screen. This light aircraft was blissfully on its way to Biggin Hill!

Many light aircraft were not equipped with radio, but even if they were, several pilots were frightened of Air Traffic Control and some aircraft owners did not wish their movements to be controlled. They did not realise how much we could help them.

My colleague of the 'white paint' episode and I tried voicing our concern over the prevailing situation through the normal channels, but without tangible results. We therefore wrote to Mr. Frank Beswick, the M.P. who had helped close the loophole in the law allowing pilots without an Instructor's Rating give flying lessons. We suggested that zones should be extended where necessary and that Terminal areas be made permanently subject to communication with Air Traffic Control. Also that the varying bases be standardized to approximately 3,000 feet which would still enable light aircraft to fly around the zones and comply safely with the low flying rules. This would help protect departing and arriving aircraft at a time when airline and executive pilots are at their busiest, completing their detailed checks.

As most of the holding patterns in the London area lay outside a Control Zone they were therefore subject to unknown traffic flying through them. The collision hazard could be reduced by the use of surveillance radar, but it was virtually impossible to separate a stack of holding aircraft from an aircraft whose height and intentions were not known. We pointed out that trooping flights , flights carrying Army or other service personnel, were carried out from Stansted, which, although it was London's third airport, had no controlled airspace or radar. Also that it was used by BOAC and BEA for training and was the base of the Civil Aviation Flying Unit which carried out the Commercial and Instrument Rating tests. All levels allocated to these aircraft gave separation from known traffic only. It took another two years for any improvement to be made. The lobby of private pilots and owners was too powerful. I had to continue the battle at a later stage when I became a member of the Air Safety Group at Westminster. Eventually the base of the London Terminal area came down, Gatwick's zone was extended and Stansted was given some controlled airspace.

....

Despite all this, by the end of 1963 I was longing to return to full-time flying. I had faith in the overworked Controllers and knew they would always do their best. That was the trouble; everyone always relied on them to do their utmost to make an outdated system work. British Air Traffic Control was regarded as second to none.

Later, as a Captain, I perhaps made a vital decision once a week or month. A Controller could do so at least once a day. I therefore applied to Freddy Laker, who was at that time Managing Director of British United Airways. He replied, saying that he had a high regard for women pilots as he had flown with them in the Air

Transport Auxiliary during the War, but that he, unfortunately, had no vacancies. However, in between seeing the boys and having them home at weekends when A.T.C. shifts permitted, I still managed to do some Dakota flights and surprisingly was asked if I would like to get it on my licence. This meant taking the written technical exam and doing a flight test.

Charles Argles was good enough to give up time to help me with the technical side, but it took three and a half months to get the required six take-offs and landings to qualify. He said he only persevered against great opposition because I was mad enough to go on the night paper flights – only receiving permission provided it did not cost the Company anything! Indeed, it was Charles who put my foot on the last rung towards becoming a full-time airline pilot.

He was sympathetic because he had become hooked on flying after joining the University Air Squadron whilst at Oxford reading Chemistry. After volunteering for the Air Force he was trained in England and Rhodesia and became a ferry pilot in the Middle East until the end of the War. He then transferred to Civil Aviation, joining Skyways in 1947 as a co-pilot on Yorks and D.C.4's, obtaining a command on Lancastrians towards the end of the Berlin Airlift. After a year in Kuwait he had joined Morton Air Services at Croydon, flying Rapides, Doves and Herons, adding Dakotas once the Company had moved to Gatwick after the closure of Croydon. He had become an Instrument Rating Examiner and as such was able to train me as a co-pilot. After overcoming even more opposition, Charles was able to have me accepted as a freelance pilot so that I was able to help out at the end of that Summer, standing in for pilots who were ill. I happily flew over fifty hours!

This whetted my appetite all the more and I applied to Morton's to become a full-time First Officer. My first application was rejected, as was my second, but my third was accepted early in December 1964, thanks to even harder work by Charles Argles, to whom I owe a very great deal. I was over the moon!

Chapter 13

Interim

I had to attend a British Women Pilots Christmas party in London the evening after I heard that I had finally been accepted as a full-time airline pilot. I delightedly told a few friends my good news, but asked them not to say anything as I had only just written my letter of resignation that Saturday morning.

Someone, however, leaked the information to the *Daily Express!*

Ironically, I had been asked by the C.A.F.U. to stand in for another pilot down at Hurn for the whole of the following week. This surprisingly had been approved by Air Traffic and I was in the middle of packing when the door bell rang. A reporter and photographer were on the door step wanting the story. They said they would do it better than anyone else. I firmly told them 'NO COMMENT' as I had nothing in writing. They departed eventually – very reluctantly.

As the boys' schools broke up for the Christmas holidays that week, Jon's on the Monday and Christopher's on the Friday, I had invited Aunty Mary to have a break in Bournemouth and look after Jon whilst I was flying. Radar target flying at the school started on a Monday afternoon so I had arranged with the Examiner, with whom I would be sharing, that I would work mornings. We were therefore able to pick Jon up from Christ's Hospital en route. I greatly enjoyed my first morning's flying, but when I landed there was a message awaiting me to phone the A.T.C.O. i/c at Gatwick. I did so to find that he could not accept my resignation. I had to write to the Secretary of the Ministry of Aviation – I sent a telegram on my way back to the hotel!

Wednesday morning's flying entailed deviating whilst doing precision approaches down to ground level. After the final landing I found the Press awaiting me – the same reporter and cameraman with back-up. I was told that Captain Morton had agreed to the release of the story. I asked to check what they had written. It was so exaggerated that I couldn't believe that Captain Morton would have approved it. I decided to phone him.

When contacted, Captain Morton replied that he was sorry but they had decided to withdraw the offer of the job. I immediately said that if it was because of the Press I would deal with them. He then asked what I was doing down at Bournemouth and when would I be returning. It was arranged that I should see him on the Friday afternoon.

He did not tell me that one of the pilots had threatened to leave if a woman joined the Company!

However, I told the Press "No story – no job!" I felt numb and could only hope that something might come of the meeting on Friday.

That evening I had a phone call from Sheila Scott, the round-the-world flyer. She had been extensively interviewed on my behalf by the Express. She told me not to worry and called the next evening to say that they had also spoken to Sir Alan Cobham.

My sagging morale was also raised by the Ministry pilots staying in the same hotel. They all stood up when I joined them for supper. This simple courtesy meant a great deal.

After finishing flying on Friday morning we packed up and I drove back to Horsham via Christopher's school. I dropped the family off at home, picked up my post and went on to Gatwick to keep my appointment with Captain Morton.

He first questioned me as to who had given me permission to fly part-time with the Company. I replied that I thought that he must have done. He then suggested that I should go back to Air Traffic Control and that, if I did so, they would compensate me. Without hesitation I said "NO"!

Immediately afterwards I thought, if need be, I would go back to flying instructing. He then said he needed to make a phone call and went out. Unable to get through he returned and asked me to wait in another office. Whilst waiting I started looking through my mail and discovered a letter from the Ministry of Aviation. It stated that although I had been cleared by my own doctor after some time off with Colitis, I needed to be examined by the Ministry Doctor before exercising the duties of a controller or pilot. In blissful ignorance I had been doing both during the previous few weeks!

When summoned back to Captain Morton's office, he just looked up at me and said, "You can tell your friends in the Press that they have won." And so I was accepted under duress and a very big black cloud!

I later heard that the Express were so incensed that they had also contacted Freddie Laker, at that time Managing Director of British

United Airways of which Morton's was an associate. I understand that he suggested it would be a good idea to reinstate me before the Press printed the story of my rejection.

I naturally felt rather awkward and dazed during the time I was working out my notice. However the controllers were kind enough to give me a farewell party and I was very touched by their presentation of a silver tray inscribed with all their signatures. Following in my Father's footsteps, the A.T.C.O. i/c finished his speech by saying 'Morton's didn't know what they were getting!'

Ironically, during my last month as a controller, I was indeed offered the post of flying the Ministry Air Traffic Examiners round the U.K. to check controllers at various airports. However, this would have only entailed about fifty hours per year, in between air traffic duties – and I wanted to fly full-time.

After the news broke, I was pestered day and night by the Press. I think my only claim to fame was that I was, probably, the first female co-pilot to be employed full-time by an airline based at a British International Airport. But I was, of course, billed as 'The First Woman Pilot'. This was despite the fact that I think ex-wartime Air Transport Auxiliary pilots Monique Agazarian and Jackie Moggeridge had been very experienced Captains for years. Since the War, Monique had been doing pleasure flying from Croydon and then Heathrow, and Jackie had flown with Channel Airways round the south coast of Britain, as well as doing many other things. I was merely, humbly and belatedly, following in their footsteps and those of all the A.T.A. and pre and post-war record breaking women pilots. However, as far as the Press was concerned, every woman pilot was 'the first!' and it continued thus for many years to come.

At that time the pressure was so great that I took my phone off its base and smothered it with a pillow! Unfortunately the Police came to the house to advise me that Reuters wanted to contact me and that my phone seemed to be out of order. I felt really guilty afterwards when their car refused to start and they had to wait 'patiently' for assistance!

In order to escape for a few hours, I decided to take the family to visit my parents in Haslemere. It was a cold wet day and the road was a ribbon of glistening grey. Just before Bucks Green I rounded a deceptively curved bend to find an oil tanker parked some 200 yards ahead with an oncoming refuse lorry approaching inexorably, preventing overtaking. My foot went down on the brake pedal –

nothing happened, and we aquaplaned straight into the back of the tanker. The deceleration was initially too sudden for our new safety belts, but they locked a second later. Aunty Mary, sitting in the front passenger seat, caught her knees on the shelf below the dashboard and bumped her head on the windscreen. My own body jack-knifed slightly so that I banged my nose against the steering wheel. The boys behind us were catapulted forwards and down behind the front seats. Poor Jon caught his mouth on the ridiculous metal safety belt guide, standing proud above my seat. Younger son Chris was uninjured, but desperate to get out in case of fire, having previously had to escape from a school one. Thank God there was no fire this time.

I leapt out of the car, terribly worried about Aunty who, shocked and stunned, was unable to move. I helped the children onto the grass alongside and ran towards the nearby house for help. The tanker driver rounded the corner of the house at that moment with the kind woman owner who immediately took the boys in. We were then able to assist Aunty from the car into her sitting room.

Dazed by the impact, we gratefully accepted the kindness shown us. I tried to clean away the blood from Jon's mouth and mop up some of the mess we were making. Someone pointed out that my nose was cut right across the tip – I had thought it was merely a nose bleed and had vaguely wondered why it hadn't stopped. A Doctor was called in and after a quick examination mercifully assured us that our injuries were not serious. Aunty Mary's knees, however, would be painful for a while due to the under skin bruising and my nose would require stitching. I was just deeply thankful that we were all still alive and will never forget the kind help given us. I learned that the unfortunate lady of the house had to cope with quite a few accidents on that corner, due to the poor camber of the road, let alone the rain.

It was only after I had managed to get my little family safely back home in a taxi that the possible repercussions dawned on me. The medical on which my job depended was in two days time. Our family Doctor put five black stitches in my nose the next day and I had to present myself to the Central Medical Establishment in London with same in situ. Perhaps the cheek of turning up like that helped me pass! As I also had to be a witness at a friend's wedding later that week, I bought a hat with a disguising veil on route.

The stitches came out the day after the wedding, but the bruising and swelling remained for another few, so that I still had to wear concealing make-up for my first official flight on the 16th January, 1965.

Chapter 14

Morton Air Services - Airline Pilot

My first official flight with Morton's was a night paper one in a Dakota to Dusseldorf with Charles Argles. All went well until we arrived when we were ushered into a hangar full of the world's press. I will never forget the blaze of light which greeted us. For the first time I knew how the Beatles must have felt! Fortunately things settled down after that but I was then worried that I might be given the sack for being a Jonah. I had three emergencies within my first six weeks!

The first was a fire warning on the port (left-hand) engine just after we had taken off from Gatwick. On the Captain's instructions, I completed the fire drill and we made a Spitfire-like approach back into land. The Fire Service was ready and waiting for us and followed us down the runway and back to the hangars. As we couldn't taxi on one engine, we were ignominiously towed backwards. On arrival it was found that a piece of metal cowling had fatigued and broken off exposing the fire wires to the exhaust. Had we kept the engine going much longer we could have had a real fire on our hands!

The second emergency was a quiet one. The starboard (right-hand) engine on another Dakota just faded away en route Dusseldorf and it was better to continue than to return, Dusseldorf being the closer.

The third was a propeller overspeed, once again in the early hours out of Gatwick. This was when I would have appreciated the all-round visibility of the Military runway lighting to help position the aircraft in the pre-dawn haze; the civil bi-directional lights were not visible downwind. After landing we were once again given an ignominious tow. I was later told that as soon as the fire crew heard my voice on the R.T. they were 'at the ready'!

However, I had had my three and the flying then calmed down and I soon became accustomed to working two or three nights in a row. The take-offs from Gatwick were scheduled for 02.40 and

02.50 GMT with the flight to Dusseldorf averaging two hours and that to Hanover two and a half. Depending on winds, the return flights could be up to thirty minutes longer. The weekend paper flights to the Channel Islands took off a little later as they averaged only an hour and we soon started bringing early flowers back on the return run.

I tried to keep a very low profile for the first six months, just concentrating on doing the job as well as I could. Nevertheless, I was so happy to be flying again that those first months of winter and spring night flights passed in a blur. It was great to be part of that special world once more and have that feeling of freedom when the wheels left the ground. Concentrating on the flying helped exclude earthly problems and prejudice.

The pilot who had threatened to leave didn't do so for a few months, and then went on to a bigger airline, the transfer having been planned before I even came on the scene. Fortunately, other pilots didn't follow suit. When I started, I think it was 25% pro, 25% not sure and only 50% somewhat anti. Even so, the odds were better than when I started in Air Traffic!

I was initially only allowed to do freight flights, but after six months these were interspersed with day-time schedule passenger flights to the Channel Isles.

On one occasion, the baggage compartment in the cockpit of the Dakota came in useful. As per programme, I had flight planned for Guernsey, but on arrival at the turning point the Captain started aiming for Jersey. He wasn't convinced until I had physically checked the luggage labels!

....

I was still under probation when I was taken aback by a letter advising me that I had been chosen to receive the inaugural I.O.P.A. – International Owner and Pilot Association – award to a Controller in Europe. This would take place in Munich and I would be flown there and back by an executive aircraft! A rather surprised Captain Morton gave me time off to attend the Conference.

It so happened that I was rostered for three night paper flights prior to the day of departure. I was therefore looking forward to relaxing as a passenger. However, the courteous Captain asked me to do him the honour of being his co-pilot and I worked harder than ever, his aircraft being a lot faster than the Dakota! It also flew much higher and when I requested flight level 170 (17,000 feet) from London instead of our usual 7,000 feet, the bemused controller asked 'Yvonne, do you really mean one seven zero?'!

I was somewhat exhausted on arrival at Munich and tried to recover before stepping out of the aircraft, but didn't have time as a welcoming committee had already reached us with a beautiful bouquet of flowers. Shortly afterwards I had to be very careful whilst trying to drink the champagne kindly offered as my silly hands shook again.

I was able to have a short rest before dinner in the hotel that evening and then spent the next day attending the interesting conference which discussed the problems of light and executive aircraft fitting in with airline traffic. The proceedings were completed on the second day with the presentation of the award, a beautifully sculptured pair of bronze hands on a plinth of black marble signifying the guarding and guiding of air traffic. I was overwhelmed and quite certain I didn't deserve it. I felt it was probably the female voice that had won the day as it had been very popular during the War, but perhaps being a pilot myself had helped. My only regret was that I didn't have time to see something of the beautiful city of Munich. However, I was fortunate enough to be able to keep the beautiful award as a new one was sculpted each following year. I treasure mine.

....

Back on the work front things improved. Having been allowed to do some passenger flights on the Dak, I was then permitted to convert to the Heron, which was just like a big Dove. After passing the technical exams and flying test, I was able to do the Swansea schedule service and the Gatwick – Alderney – Southampton services, which normally involved six sectors a day. If the weather was good, it was very pleasant to walk up to the cliff tops in Alderney and relax on the grass during our lunch break. Much better than being in the Tower!

However, the Channel weather could be tricky and for the first time in my life, I saw sea spouts one day on the sector Southampton to Alderney. We suddenly lost nearly a thousand feet in a powerful downdraft.

As aircrew we were somewhat shaken, but when we

apologised to the passengers, we found that they had enjoyed it! When the cloud base was low we were very grateful to Guernsey radar for positioning onto the approach for a radio beacon let down, which enabled us to descend to a safe height from which we would hope to see the runway lights. We were always glad when we did, otherwise we would have to divert to Guernsey and our passengers return by boat!

? Jersey

During the time I was under probation, I had worn the uniform lent me by an executive pilot friend, which I had used whilst freelancing. I had been very grateful to him, despite the comments made one day when he was taxiing past the Tower at Gatwick: "Whose trousers are you wearing today?" The look on my trainee's face had been a picture! However, after three months I was entitled to have a uniform made. I continued to use the B.U.A. hostess blouses but otherwise tried to blend in with the men as much as possible.

That summer was a very busy one. We were lucky if we had two or three days off per month. Fortunately the Sunday paper flights finished early so that I was usually able to have my boys home from school if there was an outing. On one occasion I was late back from Guernsey so had to pick Jon up still wearing my uniform. Whilst I was waiting, another mother came up to me to say how grateful she was. Apparently all her son wanted for his next birthday was an autograph book for my signature – not the expected bicycle! At least someone appreciated me. My own sons had taken it all in their stride – Mother had always been a pilot!

When I joined Morton's it was still the norm for pilots to work up to 120 hours per month and then carry on if they passed a medical. It must have been a hangover from the war years, when pilots flew day and night, all the hours necessary to protect their country. However, flying long hours year after year caused fatigue and consequently accidents. After some bad ones involving many passengers, a campaign was mounted on television by aircrew, who indeed risked their jobs by so doing. The frightened public begged their travel agents to make sure that their pilots were not over-tired. Although it would take time for legislation to be passed, the Ministry of Aviation took notice and asked airlines to restrict flying hours to 100 per month from the beginning of September 1965.

Morton's was over-committed and unable to do so immediately, but come the autumn we were each arbitrarily given a week off to make up for lost days off and reduce our flying hours. This meant that I was able to take not only a ten day holiday in Menorca at the end of September, but also have a week off visiting my Mother in South Africa during November. The holiday in Menorca turned out to be the forerunner of many in the Island and a foretaste of the future.

My Father and Nan had not had a break for seven years and had been offered the use of an apartment set into the cliff-side of the big bay of Cala en Porter, situated on the south coast. At that time, the Island did not need tourists so there were no shops in the village. Meals therefore had to be taken in the one and only hotel, which unfortunately had to close a week after their arrival due to illness of the owner. I had been invited to join them as my boys were back at school. Charles Argles and his fiancée Margaret were also interested and an apartment alongside would have been available when the three of us arrived a week later. Luckily someone in charge of a new development recommended staying in the Xuroy Hotel in Cala Alcaufar on the south eastern corner of the Island.

The Xuroy was able to take the five of us and we enjoyed a really relaxed holiday, swimming in the blue water of the creek, sunbathing on the beach, having breakfast and midday and evening drinks on the terrace, which had one of the most picturesque vistas in Menorca. The weather was perfect and we fell in love with it. We hired a taxi for one day only, grudgingly feeling we ought to see something of the rest of the Island. It was so unspoilt that we were the only people on the wide crescent beach of Arenal on the north east coast and the beautiful tree lined beach of the horseshoe bay of Cala Galdana on the south side. There wasn't even a hut of any kind, let alone a house or hotel!

Our arrival on the Island had also been one of contrasts. We had flown from Gatwick to Palma on one of B.U.A.'s newly acquired BAC1-11s. As Morton's was an associate company, we were entitled to discount fares and I was able to be up in the cockpit for the last part of the flight. I had had a panoramic view of Barcelona and then the northern mountains of Mallorca before descending rapidly into the airport of Palma and transferring to the overnight steamer, whose old-fashioned gleaming engine pistons belied the jet age. It was so peaceful. We were equally entranced by the views early next morning of the cliffs and half hidden bays and creeks of the southern coast in the lifting mist.

The passage up the long fjord-like estuary was also intriguing, expecting to see the port of Mahon round every bend and small island. The harbour itself is right at the very top with the civil side on left and the military on the right. It is famous for its deep channel approach and safety from most wind directions and was indeed used by Nelson.

The picturesque capital city of Mahon is built on a steep slope above the cliffs of the civil docking area, the architecture being a mixture of Spanish, English and French. I don't normally like cities but this one later became a favourite.

During subsequent visits we learned that because of its harbour and strategic position in the Mediterranean, Menorca had been conquered in turn by the Phoenicians, Spaniards, Moors, various pirates, the English, French, English again and finally Spaniards once more. Also that Alcaufar had been used by the English for their invasion!

The poor islanders had become adept at survival, sometimes living on birds only. They became very resilient and in 1965 Menorca was self-sufficient with no unemployment. I was even told that specialist aero-engineering had been added to the island's exports, along with production of cheese and shoes, which were exported to Europe and America. It did not need tourists, but sadly, had tourism thrust upon it.

The Island itself is divided diagonally from Mahon to Cuidadela in the north west, Cuidadela being at one time the Moorish capital, but not as picturesque as Mahon. Arabic arches remain only in one street, in front of a parade of shops.

The southern half of Menorca is flatter and more volcanic with fewer trees and the northern part is noticeably greener and hilly with fir tree woods, large fields and farm houses on top of the hills, instead of in the valleys as in the U.K. Some areas even have scenery and red earth similar to Devon and other parts look like Dorset.

The Island is a mixture of South Africa and England. There is a legend which says that it was split in half by a sea quake many centuries ago and then drifted back together again. Some years later I discovered a photograph on the wall of a bank which depicted the difference clearly.

But this time, our short holiday drew to an end all too quickly. We were sad to leave, but knew we would return. Back in

England, I promised my boys to take them to Menorca the following year.

....

Autumn came early that October and some of our passenger and paper flights were delayed due to fog and low cloud, but at least my instrument flying improved!

Pilots were only permitted to make an approach to land if the runway visibility was 600 yards or more, and then only allowed to descend to a specified height above ground level, according to the accuracy of the landing aid being used. This height was usually 200 feet for the Instrument Landing System, but could be 400 feet for a radio beacon approach. If one didn't see the ground or runway at the decision height, one had to overshoot and try again, if conditions warranted, or join the holding pattern and wait for the weather to improve. If it didn't do so within a certain time one had to divert to an alternate aerodrome. Pilots always had to carry enough fuel for these contingencies, sometimes twice as much as was required for the flight itself!

It was always satisfying if one could make a steady approach on instruments, then see the runway ahead and make a smooth landing. Unfortunately bumpy conditions and strong winds could make it uncomfortable for the passengers, especially when water on the runway necessitated a firm landing. Unless the wheels penetrated the layer of water, they would aquaplane and slide on top of the film. The brakes would then be useless and the aircraft could over-run the runway or be blown sideways off it. It was better to suffer a firm landing!

....

It indeed came as a surprise when I was suddenly given the week off early in November, to make up for the excess hours flown during September. As Jon and Chris were in the middle of their school terms I was unable to do anything with them so, on the spur of the moment, decided to visit my mother in South Africa. Although she had visited us twice in England, I had not seen her for three years. I could fly on British United's VC10 from Gatwick to Nairobi and would then hitch a lift with another airline. My mother was overjoyed as neither of my sisters had been able to visit her since leaving for America and England. Fortunately Ian and Norah Selwyn were still in Kenya and were kind enough to offer to help me on my way. It was all organised very quickly.

On checking in at Gatwick, I was asked to talk to a lady who had been saving for years to visit her son in Mozambique, but had taken fright and couldn't bring herself to board the aircraft. I explained that I was on my way to see my Mother and told her how long I had been flying and how careful the pilots were. She calmed down and decided to come provided I sat next to her. She held my hand tightly on take-off, but wanted to know why I wasn't flying it! She settled down when we levelled off and was able to enjoy the evening meal and then go to sleep. I found it impossible to sleep sitting in my seat, so asked to go up to the cockpit. The crew were very pleasant and were happy to explain the details of their special aeroplane. Having flown the route very recently, the Captain invited me to stay up front to watch Hailey's Comet against the background of sunrise over the Sahara. It was the most fantastic sight, a Christmas star with its long bright trail travelling across the red and yellow of the desert dawn. I will never forget it.

The lady was still asleep when I returned to the cabin. I was sad that she hadn't seen it, but the view from a side window could not have been as beautiful as the privileged one from the cockpit. The rest of the flight became interesting when the monotony of the desert sands gave way to savannah type country with a few trees and several animals on the move. Our stop in Salisbury, Rhodesia, was lengthened by having to wait for an engine to be changed due to a bird having been ingested during our approach to land. Despite the delay in the really hot sunshine, my lady took it all in her stride. She had become a seasoned traveller!

I was met in Nairobi by Ian and driven to their home on the outskirts of the city, where a warm welcome and meal awaited me. On checking with the airport, we found that there was a British Airways freight flight passing through on its way to Johannesburg at 03.00 hours. It seemed a possibility so we went out to the airport but were told that they were not allowed to carry a passenger. Although disappointed, we discovered that a Scandinavian Airlines DC 8 was leaving at 08.00 hours and was only permitted to carry half the normal number of passengers to South Africa; fortunately there was room for one more!

After returning back to their house for a little more sleep and an early breakfast, I was able to get airborne again in luxury. The weather was really clear en route and the Captain flew the aircraft gently round Mount Kilimanjaro, giving us an impressive view of the crater. Little did I realise that my granddaughter, Samantha, would climb both Mount Kenya and Kilimanjaro in the year 2002! The rest of the flight was pleasant and uneventful and I was able to relax in between visiting the cockpit once more. We had to hold on arrival at Johannesburg so also had a good view of the gold mines whilst circling. I tried to advise my mother of my delayed time of arrival, but there was a mix-up and she had gone home to Pretoria by the time I reached the terminal. After searching in vain, I phoned her flat and caught her just as she entered. She returned immediately! We made the most of the few days I was with her and I caught up with relations and friends I had not seen for nearly twenty years.

Pretoria is built in a wide, open valley and I was pleased that my Mother's flat overlooked the beautiful Union Buildings with its sloping gardens for which the city is famous. These buildings are one of the three seats of Government in South Africa.

I was also glad that she still had her faithful maid and companion, Rosie, to look after her. Rosie came in each day and mothered both of us, and it was decided that I would bring the boys out for a holiday over the next Easter. My only regret was that I had missed the full glory of October's Jacaranda time when the trees in the city streets and gardens displayed their wonderful mass of lilac blue foxglove-like blooms. All that was left was a violet blue haze. My return journey was broken again in Nairobi, where I stayed once more with Ian and Norah, and ate all the fresh pineapple I could in a day. I wasn't to enjoy this luxury again until I was invited as a guest to a Woman of the Year Luncheon at the Savoy in London a year later!

My flight from Nairobi to England was in an East African Airlines Comet. Had I known that I would one day fly this wonderful aircraft, I would have asked to spend much more time in the cockpit. It was the very first of the jet airliners. My Father had flown on one of its early flights and had loved it. Even after the initial accidents, due to window design, he had said he would fly on it again immediately it was brought back into service.

....

Just before Christmas, Morton's were asked to fly an urgently required piece of BAC 1-11 equipment down to Lisbon. I was the co-pilot on the Heron and we took off in the early hours in order to reach Lisbon by 08.00.

All went well until we called in at Bordeaux for fuel, where the Met. Officer told us there was a possibility of fog at Lisbon not clearing until later in the day. With plenty of fuel we decided to continue, but were unlucky. The fog did not clear until much later. Together with several other aircraft we diverted to Oporto up the coast. Here our luck changed as we fortunately encountered a Portuguese Airline crew who would be returning to Lisbon as soon as possible and would take the equipment for us. This enabled us to have a rest in a hotel before flying back to Gatwick that same evening. I remember thinking what a contrast the limpid sky and gently warm sun was to the England we had left behind that morning. The return flight was pleasant until we came up to the English Channel where we hit a vicious front that was passing through. The strong winds and heavy rain did not make for a comfortable approach and I had to use almost all the runway to put the aircraft down!

We flew over nine hours that day and, to my surprise, I found that I had flown almost nine hundred hours during the year.

As usual Aunty Mary was with us for the school holidays and Christmas, which was a really good one. There was so much to look forward to.

....

The winter snows of 1966 affected Europe more than Britain. On one of our paper flights to Dusseldorf we were forced to fly so low that we had to use German radar to guide us round some hills.

On another occasion, en route to Switzerland, we tried to climb up to 10,000 feet in an attempt to get above the weather, struggling to reach it only in time to come down! After several murky flights, we finally made it and it was a joy to suddenly climb out above the cloud into the clear blue sky above. I felt like looping the loop! It is always fascinating to fly just above the layer of white cotton wool cloud; so white in the sunshine, so grey down below.

With the Spring came Easter and our visit to South Africa. It was a great success and made really memorable by the kindness of a family friend who drove us to the Kruger Park Game Reserve – my first time as well. As it was autumn in South Africa, the dried grasses sometimes made the animals difficult to see, but we saw most of them, including elephants and the white rhinoceros. Lions were the exception – we had to catch up with them in their bush enclave in the Pretoria Zoo!

During that summer, I flew to Bournemouth again. Morton's had obtained a contract from the Atomic Energy Authority to fly their specialists from Manchester via Abingdon to Hurn, Mondays to Fridays, returning via the same route of an evening. This meant positioning up to Manchester on a Sunday and then back to Gatwick the following Saturday, and spending most of the week-days in Bournemouth.

A Heron was used for this service and we were rostered in turn for it. I would take the opportunity to slip up to the tower to say "hello" to the Air Traffic Controllers and also visit the garage owner, who had looked after my car so well whilst I was doing radar target flying and clocking up an impressive mileage, with journeys up to Stansted for night flying as well. His kind wife would provide a welcoming lunch.

One morning while climbing the steps up to the tower, I saw the Training Officer who had failed me, coming down. I didn't feel too comfortable, but he passed me, only to stop, turn around and then to my amazement say "I'm sorry, I underestimated you". All I could reply was, "Thank you".

Another surprise awaited me that summer: I was finally checked out on the Dove again, but only as a co-pilot. The Dove was used for executive flights and just before my summer holiday we were chartered to fly Shirley Bassey up to Blackpool for a one night performance. The weather was somewhat bumpy on the way up and the poor passengers were rather queasy on arrival. This, however, did not affect Shirley Bassey's performance that evening. She held that audience spellbound for the whole of the second half! I had seen her briefly on television and could not believe the sheer ebullience and dynamism of her 'live' performance. Unfortunately my young Captain was sickening for 'flu so was not able to enjoy the show as much as I did, and I had to fly the Dove back to Gatwick.

....

On returning home at 03.00 hours I found the lights on in my flat and Aunty Mary waiting up for me. There had been an accident. Jon's right arm had been scalded by water just off the boil. He had, thank goodness, put it under cold water immediately and she had then smothered it with Acriflex burns cream before bandaging it. He was asleep when I arrived, but woke at 06.00 and came in to show me the damage. I was horrified when I saw the grey flesh and realised that the arm would have to be seen by a doctor. I was so tired and shocked that I asked Charles Argles to take him to the hospital for me. I was afraid that I would pass out en route.

We were due to leave for Menorca that afternoon and the Doctor was scathing, commenting that the arm would need to be dressed three times a day and Jon would not be able to swim for a least a week. Knowing that there was a good doctor on the Island, I decided to go ahead.

My Father was flying out with us and Nan was following on. Very sadly he had been diagnosed with lung cancer and had been treated with radio-therapy, so was not very strong. Our flights had been booked through a travel agency and it wasn't until we had taken off from Gatwick that I checked the onward inter-island tickets. I found that we were booked on the first flight the next morning and would have to stay overnight in Palma. Fortunately the airport staff were able to find us accommodation, but I had to cope with Jon's arm.

On arrival in Menorca we went straight to the Doctor's surgery and he was able to reassure us that all would be well. A burns cream similar to Acriflex was prescribed and Jon was swimming within four days! It was a happy family holiday which the boys thoroughly enjoyed, spending most of their time in and out of the water, whilst the adults swam farther each day. We took a boat trip along the south coast, calling at one bay for a swim and another for a picnic. We also took a boat trip up the estuary to see the fireworks on the water in celebration of the Mahon Fiesta. They were, indeed, spectacular!

During that holiday I noticed that the attentive terrace waiter was particularly kind to all the children, buying them drinks and ice-creams out of his own pocket. They were far more expensive than our adult ones. At that time the price of a gin was something like 4p, a brandy 5p and a Coca-Cola 10p! His name was Miguel Sintes and I learned that he had been studying to be a doctor when the Spanish Civil War broke out. He worked as a paramedic in the Medical Corps throughout the War, but due to lack of finance, was unable to complete his training as a doctor afterwards. His Father had been shot by troops loyal to Franco. When the War finished he initially remained on the mainland, working in Madrid and later, Bilbao, returning to Menorca when his Mother became ill, only to find there were no vacancies in the small island hospital. He had therefore taken any temporary job available and had ended up on the terrace of the Xuroy Hotel! At the end of the holiday he asked if he could write to me – and this began a friendship which later blossomed.

....

During the following autumn I was asked to join the Air Safety Group which met at the House of Commons once a month under the chairmanship of Eric Lubbock, MP. I had been approached by Nancy Cox, the wife of Frank Cox, a British United Airways Captain. Nancy had been a stewardess and had risked her job by appearing on television at the time of the campaign to reduce flying hours. Having been an Air Traffic Controller, I was asked to keep a watching brief on current and future procedures. This enabled me to keep up my campaign for safer airspace around the London airports. We eventually met with the Minister of State, as well as representatives of aviation departments and I was able to detail my concerns about the safety of aircraft climbing up to and descending from airways. I pointed out that the Standard Departure and Approach procedures restricted aircraft in the 'free for all' area from 2,000 feet to 5,000 feet – the levels used by several unknown light aircraft. I suggested that an increase in the size of the compulsory radio communications area would improve everyone's safety at a time when pilots were busiest with their various checks. All that was necessary was radio contact between all the aircraft in the vicinity and the controller. Light aircraft without radio could use defined corridors.

Unfortunately there was still a lot of opposition from private pilots, who wanted their freedom and didn't realise how much the Air Traffic Controllers could help them. It would have helped if an RT licence was made a necessary inclusion in the Private Pilots Licence. Amendments were, however, finally made to the airspace around London. I didn't know it at the time, but have since been told that the procedure to change any law through Parliament usually took at least two years!

Christmas that year was a quiet one as my Father's health had continued to deteriorate. Very, very sadly he died on the 11th January, 1967. I loved him so much and was with him at the time, but could not have wished for life to be extended in his weakened and tired body. His soul was freed to continue. My dear step-mother, Nan, was bereft and would have liked to follow him, but I persuaded her that we needed her and that, if she was still here, there must be a reason.

Apart from continuing to help us and write her beauty and other magazine articles, as well as an informative book, she quite soon found that a nearby boarding school needed extra accommodation for their girls and ended up with three girls at a time to stay with her. She had a wonderful rapport with teenagers and there was always a queue of girls wanting to stay with her.

When she had finally had to give up hope of having her own children, a wise woman had told her that if she opened up her heart she could have the biggest family she could wish for – and so it proved. She added the school girls to the list of others she had 'adopted' when they had been in need of help. She also fulfilled some of her early hopes of working in the medical field by becoming an Assistant Matron at the school. However, immediately after my Father's death, Nan's thyroid misbehaved and her eyes were affected by shingles. At the same time that she had to go into St, Thomas' Hospital for treatment, I had to have a small operation which affected me more than usual – so we were a fine pair!

I was initially able to convalesce with my good friends Jock and Betty Hunter, and later was invited to stay a week with an Air Traffic Controller and his kind wife down at Plymouth, while Nan recuperated with her best friend in Launceston.

After his boarding school had been burned down, my younger son Chris had stayed with Nan and my Father for a year whilst attending a nearby school as a day boy. However, he had been accepted by King Edward's Boarding School, Witley during 1966, so we fortunately didn't have to worry about his being cared for solely by Nan's elder sister, Norrie, who had lived with them since the death of their parents.

Not long after returning to work, I received a most unexpected and very welcome surprise. I was advised that I was one of four winners of the Amelia Earhart Memorial Scholarship of $700 to help me obtain the British Airline Transport Licence. This is a scholarship awarded annually by the Ninety-Nines International Organisation of Women Pilots, which was brought into being by this famous record breaking pilot. The organisation was started in 1929 when over a hundred licensed women pilots in America were invited by Amelia to a meeting in a hangar on Curtis Field, Long Island. She became its first President and named it after the 99 women who were able to attend that first meeting. It has since spread world-wide and there are now thousands of members, including the most famous women pilots.

The aims of the Ninety-Nines are to promote a close relationship among women pilots and help them in any way that can benefit aviation and world-wide friendship. The scholarship was instigated in 1940 as a tribute to Amelia, who accepted no favours because of her sex, and proved time and time again that she could compete on equal terms with men in aviation. She broke record after record, but never counted her success as personal glory. Tragically, both she and her navigator disappeared mysteriously during her last round the world flight. Her modesty and quiet determination inspired this scholarship, which is aimed at helping women obtain professional qualifications. She will always be remembered.

I had been a founder member of the British Section of the Ninety-Nines in 1964 and had been Chairman of the scholarship committee, when our candidate, Janet Ferguson, had won through to later become an international ferry pilot. After handing over to Elizabeth Overbury, another airline pilot, I was persuaded by Sheila Scott, the Governor of our British Section and British record breaking pilot, to apply myself. I needed my normal leave to be with my sons during their holidays and could not afford to take unpaid leave to study for the Airline Transport Pilots Licence. The Scholarship enabled me to do this.

I was invited to attend the 1967 Convention in Washington to receive the award in person. After being approached by Elizabeth, Captain Morton gave his permission and the British Section offered me a loan from their special fund to help me with the necessary expenses. BOAC also kindly gave me a discount flight – after all, I had been a stewardess with them! After checking in for the BOAC 707 flight to New York, I ascertained the whereabouts of the crew before they went out to the aircraft. I explained that I had been an Air Traffic Controller and understood that American procedures differed somewhat from the British and asked if it would be possible to be in the cockpit for a short while after we crossed into American Airspace.

I was indeed invited up front during the early part of the flight, shown the instrumentation and handed the 707 Flight Manual to take back to read in the cabin. I don't know what the nearby passengers thought, but I learned something about the rolling tendencies of the aircraft under certain conditions! I also spent the last part of the flight in the cockpit and found that en route position reporting was done more by electronic means than voice. On approaching our airport, we were advised that there was a multiplicity of military traffic in the area. Including those of a supernumerary Captain, five pairs of eyes very carefully scanned that area! We were cleared for a visual approach on to a non-instrument runway and, in the hazy visibility, the lead-in lights were not easy to see, the first one being unserviceable. Nonetheless, a safe landing was made.

When we reached the terminal, I was treated like a V.I.P. I was met by a Senior Aviation Official and whisked through Immigration and Customs to be welcomed by waiting Ninety-Nines. I was taken to a pleasant flat for the afternoon and then returned to the Airport to meet some well-known Australian pilots, three of us being taken by our overnight hostess to her beautiful home in the green undulating countryside outside the city. Helicopter flights were laid on for the next morning and the views were, of course, stupendous. It was probably the best way to see New York.

The Convention itself did not start until two days later so, instead of flying straight on to Washington, I was able to make a detour to visit a South African friend – he who had helped me with my matric maths! He had obtained a good job in Syracuse and was living with his Scandinavian wife and family in a lovely peaceful area. Their pretty low white house was set in the middle of extensive green grass which sloped down gently towards a small river boundary on one side and trees on the other.

His wife kindly drove me to the Airport the next morning for my flight to Washington, but we were stopped en route by the police doing an extensive check on the serviceability of the car, as was their custom. I nearly missed the flight, but was greatly impressed by the speed my baggage was taken from me and I was whisked on board. The aircraft called in at Boston, by which time I had regained my equilibrium and wrote a note to the Captain on the menu I had saved, asking whether I could come up to the cockpit. His answer was: "Come into my parlour, said the spider to the fly!".

The crew were very friendly and typical of American hospitality, the Captain invited me to have a meal with his family, if I could escape from the Convention for an evening. I was, indeed able to do so and greatly enjoyed their relaxed company.

On arrival at Washington, I was checked in at the Convention Centre and then taken to the home of my very pleasant hosts. They could not have been kinder and we still keep in touch, despite the fact that a pilot friend phoned me at 03.00 one night whilst I was staying with them, from the other side of the continent! It was he who had lent me "Teach Yourself To Fly" in the first place – suitably annotated with his own cartoons. He, of all people, should have known better!

The business part of the Convention was conducted during the mornings with annual reports being given by the many sections. I was officially deputising for our Governor, Sheila Scott, who was unable to attend as she was in the middle of a record breaking flight to South Africa. Ideas for the improvement of the 99s contribution to aviation were discussed in detail. More painting of airfield names on top of hangars was encouraged, this being much more helpful than two letters in the signals square, i.e. 'B.F.'! Every possible support should continue to be given to the National Air Education Programme, Wing Scouts, Civil Air Patrol, as well as fund raising towards providing the scholarships for women working in aviation to advance their professional skills. New sections should be encouraged world-wide and women's air races sponsored. Interspersed with the Amelia Earhart Award Luncheon were visits to the Smithsonian Institution, Aviation Museum and the White House.

I will always remember the Museum for its fantastic display of aviation history from its very inception, and the White House for its display of the beautiful dinner services introduced by each President's wife. I particularly liked the royal blue and gold motif.

The Convention ended with a superb banquet on the 30th June, at which five continents were represented. Fortunately my dear step-mother had lent me an appropriate dress! A statement by Vice President Hubert H. Humphrey was read, welcoming visitors

from all over the world in the United Nations proclaimed
'International Tourist Year'. The Ninety-Nines were also praised
for their role in strengthening friendship and understanding
worldwide. Among the memorabilia give us was a beautifully
embossed copy of the poem 'High Flight' by John Gillespie Magee
Jr., which had always meant so much to me.

A surprise awaited us the next day: a visit to the John F.
Kennedy Space Centre had been arranged. We were collected by
a NASA aircraft and flown down to Cape Canaveral, Florida,
renamed Cape Kennedy. We were booked into a hotel situated on
a narrow sandy peninsular. All we wanted was a refreshing swim
in the sea but, with a thunderstorm threatening, found it to be like
a hot bath and rapidly retreated to the air-conditioned bar. Here
we happily had the opportunity to relax and talk to one another.
I discovered that a South African, almost namesake who was
staying at the same hotel, Yvonne van den Dool, (mine having
been van den Hoek), had at one time nearly been mistaken for me
when she had been interviewed for an executive pilot's position.
She was asked why she was applying when she already had a job
in England?! Fully qualified she had wanted to become an airline
pilot, but South African Airways were not yet accepting women.
She had also applied to the Military, but it took both of them many
years to appreciate the fact that women were as good as men. We
discovered that we had many other interests in common and have
remained friends every since.

It was also very interesting to hear why other women had
learned to fly. There were representatives from Australia, Brazil,
Canada, Greece, India, Morocco, Netherlands, Pakistan and the
Philippines, as well as South Africa. Many said they had taken it
up to overcome a personal tragedy, such as the death of a husband
or child. As someone said, 'flying is much better than tranquilizers
– you don't have to lie down and wait, you have to get up and do
it!' One has to concentrate solely on flying the aircraft, and the
distance above the ground diminishes the pain.

Whilst in Washington, I had also been greatly impressed by two
very famous women, an American and a Brazilian, both in charge
of their nation's simulator training for military as well as civil
pilots. They had taken over from men during the Second World
War and had remained in charge afterwards. They had indeed
received many military and civil awards. The actual visit to the

Space Centre was fantastic.

My abiding memory of Launch Complex 39 is the Rocket Assembly Building which provided such an incredible contrast to the low flat expanse of the Merritt Island landscape. The 525-foot building housed four assembly bays and looked half its height. The only way to realise its magnitude was to see a tiny human being standing in front of the giant crawler tracks of the adjacent transporter which would take the completed Apollo/Saturn V rocket and spacecraft to the launch pad. One hardly noticed the 210-foot lower bay building alongside, which contained eight preparation and check out cells for the upper stages of the Saturn V rocket, nor the vital four-storey Launch Control Centre from which all phases of the launch operation at Complex 39 were controlled.

When shown the rocket/launch vehicle being assembled in one of the high bays, one still could not absorb its magnitude or the fact that it would take the American Astronauts to the moon. One couldn't believe the height of the 446-foot Mobile Launcher, standing on its six 22-foot high pedestals. With its nine swing arms it served both as an assembly platform inside the bay and as a launch platform at the pad. The astronauts would enter the spacecraft via the top swing arm, the others being used to carry vital propellant, electrical and data links. They also permitted catwalk access to the vehicle during the final phase of countdown and would swing rapidly away during the launch.

Once the launch vehicle and spacecraft had been thoroughly checked and prepared, the huge transporter moving on four double track crawlers would slide under the Mobile Launcher inside the building and transfer it with its precious load to the launch site three and a half miles away. It would travel at 1 mile per hour along a specially constructed crawl way which withstood the equivalent stress of forty jetliners landing at the same time on a runway! The launch pad itself was an incredibly reinforced concrete hardstand which incorporated a 700,000 pound rocket nozzle flame deflector. Final servicing at the launch site would be provided by the Mobile Service Structure which would be removed a few hours prior to launch.

The display of Museum Mercury and Gemini artefacts also seemed unreal. Project Mercury placed a manned spacecraft in orbital flight around the earth and proved that human beings could respond and cope with the unexpected, as well as eat and drink while weightless. Gemini was the intermediate step towards manned lunar landings, proving that man can perform effectively during extended periods in space, both within and outside the spacecraft, developing rendezvous and docking techniques and perfecting controlled re-entry and landing procedures. Explorer meteorological and communications satellites were also launched from the other pads at the Space Centre, all adding to the gain of new knowledge.

Our only regret was that we were unable to meet any astronauts. Had I been younger and without ties I might have volunteered to become one myself!

The flights back to Washington and New York were uneventful, except that we had to hold for quite a while at J.F.K. and I nearly missed my return British Airways flight to the U.K., the taxi driver in between the terminals being somewhat disgruntled because I didn't have much change left for a tip!

I will never forget that wonderful visit to the U.S.A. and cannot thank the Americans enough for their warm hospitality.

....

Back home, life returned to normal and I enjoyed flying once more. Shortly after returning I bought the Airline Transport Licence (A.T.P.L.) postal course from Avigation, but as it was the start of the summer season did not have much time for studying until the winter. By this time Mortons had obtained a service from Gatwick to Ostend, departing in the morning and returning the same evening. A hotel was provided for a rest during the day, but on one occasion I flew with an ex-A.T.A. (War Air Transport Auxiliary) Captain who was an intrepid photographer and explorer. We took the Metro into Brussels and he showed me many places of interest, including the flower market, the Boy Statue and Judicial Buildings. We walked in without permission and wandered into various courts. I expected to be arrested at any minute but we somehow escaped!

We flew together on a number of occasions, one of them being a weekend charter flight to Scotland. On approach into Prestwick Airport he suddenly grabbed his camera and said "You have control" whilst he took photos of the beautiful liquid sunset! We were in Scotland for a couple of days so hired a car to drive round Loch Lomond and other Lochs. En route to the castle south of

Prestwick we experienced the Electric Brae, where the car stopped going downhill and kept on climbing uphill with power off! The Heron and Dove charter flights made a pleasant change from the normal schedule services and the night paper flights.

....

My sons had been impressed and envious when I told them about the Space Centre. I was fortunately able to compensate a little by taking them to Menorca during their summer holidays. This time we flew direct and instead of the Hotel Xuroy, stayed with Nan in Casita Teresa, the cottage bought for Nan and my Father's retirement. Sadly my Father had not lived long enough to enjoy it, but we were able to appreciate it for many years to come. The Casita was situated at the top of Alcaurfar and was only five minutes from the creek. The boys were now old enough to go down on their own to fish and swim. Nan and I would join them in time for lunch in the Hotel. Miguel spoilt them with drinks and ice creams and kept an eye on them. He also came to visit us and for the first time since Eric's death made me laugh involuntarily. As far as the boys were concerned it wasn't a really good holiday unless we had a thunderstorm at least once, and the electricity failed so that candles would have to be lit. Following a storm they also enjoyed the waves breaking over the 'aircraft carrier', the large flat rock at the entry to the creek. Incredibly they were able to catch some really good photos. On one occasion half the water in the creek was actually sucked out before rushing back in!

Back home again the autumn brought its own mixture of storms. One caused the little stream around the perimeter of Gatwick Airport to flood and inundate part of the only runway, slowly but surely. It happened during the boys half-term holiday and whilst I was doing a series of flights to the Channel Islands. Our Heron was able to land on the shortened runway during the afternoon, but by the evening the runway was closed to all traffic and we were diverted to London's main airport, Heathrow. We were handled by British Airways and I rather enjoyed walking through their briefing room in uniform. It was still not their policy to employ women pilots!

As Jon and Chris were spending the few days with Aunty Mary in her flat in Southall near Heathrow, I was able to take them by surprise and ended up sleeping on a stretcher bed in her sitting room. Gatwick remained closed for another day and night so we had some extra time together and they returned with me the following day, giving Aunty Mary her first ever flight, fortunately in sunshine.

However, an extra evening charter flight in a Dakota to Belfast, Northern Ireland was in cloud all the way there and half way back. But then we suddenly shot out into the clear night sky. There was no moon, but the stars were brilliant and the small clusters of lights down below looked like diamonds on velvet. Flying to the west of Heathrow we could see a few aircraft manoeuvring on the ground, their lights like sparkling gems. How I wished people frightened of flying could see the sky and earth blending in the beauty and serenity of that night. However, later in the winter the ice which suddenly formed at dawn over our parking area at Dusseldorf prevented us from taxiing the Dak over the skating rink to the runway. We had to return very carefully to our parking position and wait for at least an hour!

In between flying I tried studying for the A.T.P.L. at home but soon realized that I needed expert assistance. Using the money from the Amelia Earhart Scholarship I took unpaid leave to attend the Sir John Cass College in London early that December in 1967.

During that fortnight I was kindly invited by Jock and Betty Hunter to stay with them so I wouldn't need to worry about feeding myself. I travelled by train from Stansted to London each weekday and picked Jock's brains of an evening and over the weekend. Fortunately there was an instructor at the College who realized that many of us had been wartime children who had lost out on Maths. He had written out the basics of Algebra on two foolscap pages and for the first time in my life I understood why one put the figures from top to bottom or vice versa. If only I had been told early in my youth I would have had far less trouble. I had only passed exams by memorizing examples.

The pass marks for airline exams were very high, mainly 70 to 80%. I managed to pass all but one at my first attempt in March 1968, studying up to the last minute in the tube on the way in. I was lucky the second time, despite the invigilator coming up behind me in the middle of the algebraic question saying "I'm sorry Mrs Pope, the one thing we can't provide is an icebag for your fevered brow!"

Chapter 15

British Airline Pilots Association

Many of the Morton's pilots did not belong to the British Airline Pilots Association, B.A.L.P.A., but suddenly decided it could be a good idea to do so. Unfortunately no-one wanted to be Chairman of the Pilots Local Council. Already a member, I was 'elected' for the job!

Today, BALPA represents well over 75% of all the fixed wing pilots and helicopter aircrew based in the UK - as well as many working overseas. The Association has a membership of over 10,000 professional flight crew, working in companies large and small. BALPA works with the Civil Aviation Authority, the Department for Transport, the Department of Trade and Industry and many other bodies where the voice of 'the pilot' is needed.

BALPA was one of the founder members of IFALPA, the International Federation of Airline Pilots Associations, which co-ordinates the views and opinions of well over 100,000 flight crew around the globe.

After being the most unwanted addition to the Company, I found myself negotiating small improvements to the pilots' working conditions! I also had to attend various meetings at B.A.L.P.A. Headquarters in Hayes, near Heathrow. As I was particularly interested in Air Safety I became a member of that Group. Amongst several aspects of safety, which included improvements to navigational aids, the Group was trying to adopt American legislation regulating pilots working hours according to the routes flown – short, medium or long haul.

The departure and arrival sections of a flight normally require the most concentration, not only the actual take-off and landing but often the complex routing and speed control required for noise abatement over built-up areas. Many short flights a day are more tiring than fewer medium ones or one or two long haul.

Not only flying time, but duty time on the ground, must also be taken into consideration. Preparation before a flight involves checking the weather forecast for the route, destination/s and alternate/s, the flight plan details and the uplift of fuel according to the forecast winds and passenger loads. Although the ground engineers check the aircraft thoroughly at base, the pilots still have to do an external and internal check, including the setting up of instruments in the cockpit. These checks are also required during turnarounds away from base.

Therefore, working a duty, day or night, consisted of time in the air and on the ground, and adequate rest time between duty periods is very important. Tiredness can kill passengers, crew and people on the ground.

B.A.L.P.A. wished to negotiate better conditions of employment for pilots of the independent companies to bring them into line with BOAC and BEA. In order to do so, six months notice of terminating a current 'Agreement for Service' had to be given before being able to negotiate a new agreement. When Alan Bristow took over from Freddie Laker as Managing Director of British United Airways he seized the opportunity to say that in the absence of an agreement, he would not negotiate and would offer 'a personal contract' to all B.U.A. pilots. If it was not signed within seven days he would close the Company down. The personal contract gave dictatorial powers to Bristow at the expense of the pilots' previous one. This was despite the fact that legally the previous agreement of service had to continue in force until a new one was negotiated.

His persuasive tactics included phoning wives to ask them how they would feel if their husbands lost their employment, also meeting pilots at the end of a long flight to tell them that other comrades had signed so they should do so too!

Meetings with the pilots were held at which I understand the language was incredibly basic; even those who were present were surprised. Eventually a strike was called by B.A.L.P.A., which I supported, but few of the Morton's pilots were keen to do so. I was told to think of my family – although Captain Morton had been a founder member of B.A.L.P.A.!

It was intended that the associate companies, Mortons and

those based at the outstations of Southend, Lydd, Isle of Man, Blackpool and the Channel Islands should be separated from B.U.A. at Gatwick so that the main company could be sold to the Corporations. However, all the pilots of the associate companies would also have to sign his personal contract or lose their jobs.

As Pilots Local Council Chairman of Mortons, I organized several meetings with our pilots, some of which were attended by senior B.A.L.P.A. officials from Headquarters. I sent a résumé of the meetings to all the other airlines I could think of and was indeed very grateful to the Meteorological Officers at Gatwick who were good enough to do the photocopying for me.

Alas, it was to no avail. The pilots were very concerned for their families and careers, and I ended up being the only one within Mortons who would not sign! I was therefore given three months notice by the new Chief Pilot at the beginning of October. It must have been rather embarrassing to have me around, so I was called into his office after two months and told that he knew I must be looking for another job so they would release me, but pay me for the last month!

The few B.U.A. pilots who held out against duress were vindicated when the dispute, having been through the unsuccessful arbitration of the National Joint Council, was referred by the President of the Board of Trade to the Industrial Court, despite the fact that it took nineteen months and 21 sessions to rule in favour of B.A.L.P.A.!

In 1972 a new negotiated 'Agreement of Service' for B.U.A. Pilots was agreed. Thus all independent pilots in the U.K. were given the opportunity, under British law in consultation with B.A.L.P.A. and Management, to achieve equal status with the Corporations if they did comparable work on similar aircraft with overall conditions of employment no less favourable.

However, this did not prevent the non-signers from being victimized in the interim period, nor did it completely compensate for the stress and anxiety caused to the pilots and their families, especially as pilots were advised to sign the individual contract to protect their employment with B.U.A. during that time.

Although I had thought no-one would want to employ me after my efforts against the personal contract, I had indeed applied to Dan-Air. As luck would have it, the Dan-Air B.A.L.P.A. pilots' local chairman, Captain Seafield Grant walked in the door just after I had finished filling in the application form. We had met at emergency meetings at Headquarters, and he took me by the arm straight into the office of the somewhat surprised Chief Pilot, Captain Atkins, saying 'I am sure we can find Yvonne a job'! Very fortunately, another co-pilot on Dakotas down at Bristol was needed from the beginning of the next year.

I was thus able to have the whole of December off and gratefully escaped to Menorca for ten days all on my own, before the boys broke up for the Christmas holidays.

Chapter 16

Dan-Air - Dakota
And Ambassador

I started with Dan-Air on the 1st January 1969, and was checked out on the Dakota by Captain Pat Falconer, who was a legend in his own right. He had become an instructor after training in America and his civil and military flying on Dakotas amounted to over 14,000 hours. He had also founded Avigation, which specialized in providing postal courses for the Commercial and Airline Transport Licenses, as well as tuition at his school in Ealing. As with so many other pilots, I had used Avigation to gain both my licences!

On our way out to the aircraft he said 'I do hope you are not going to offer me a banana!' After a previous check flight, he was just about to give his considered opinion when the lady concerned had reached into her flight bag and offered a banana! Fortunately, I didn't need one, but on being offered one, still have flashbacks!

Dan-Air operated schedule service passenger flights from Bristol via Cardiff to Liverpool and alternately on to Newcastle and return on weekdays. These were interspersed with occasional charter flights to St Athan, Hawarden, Manchester, Ouston, Amsterdam, Jersey and the Isle of Man, only a few being over weekends. I was therefore mostly able to return home to Horsham at weekends and see something of my sons when they had an outing from school. I didn't mind driving at night because there was less traffic, leaving Bristol Friday evening and returning Sunday night the journey taking about two and a half hours

Initially I found a Bed and Breakfast place near the airport, but another pilot and his wife were then kind enough to put me up until I found something more permanent. Whilst looking, I remembered seeing a caravan on the grassy slope behind the B&B. Having enjoyed living in one, I asked if it was available. I was lucky, and Elsie Williams, who ran the B&B, and her husband Derek, who ran the adjoining Jet Garage, became good friends.

Derek introduced me to a nearby village shop where Sherry was available from the barrel.

He once saw me with two bottles when I was expecting visitors over a weekend. He swore he saw the caravan hiccup down the slope! I also remember being able to beat the cold of early mornings by falling out of bed to light the gas oven before making a cup of tea!

Every flight is slightly different so that it is never boring. The satisfaction lies in doing the job as well as one can and keeping to schedules as closely as possible, despite weather or other problems.

However, we were all thwarted on one occasion by a heavy snowfall which kept us on the ground at Liverpool for two days. Fortunately, friends I had met in Menorca lived not far away and offered me their hospitality. I ended up staying two nights with them, leaving the poor Captain in an hotel on his own as the roads became almost impassable.

On another occasion we became the unwitting cause of a near problem for another pilot. The registration of our aircraft was G.AMPP, Golf Alpha Mike Papa Papa, but the air traffic controllers normally used the last words of the International Alphabet after first contact. We were in the circuit when the other pilot, having flown a long distance, joined with his legs crossed, only to hear the further shortened 'P.P.' being given preference – he thought, due to the woman's voice!

As I had only recently joined Dan-Air, I was unable to take leave over Easter. However, Jock and Betty, who had fallen in love with Menorca, were able to do so and kindly invited Jon and Chris to join them and their son Andrew in Casita Teresa.

I was able to see them off from Luton in a beautiful Dan-Air Comet. I heard that the boys enjoyed themselves, at one time leading a crocodile of youngsters down to the local café bar to buy ice-creams and coca-cola or orange Fanta. When they returned it was found that the elder ones had requested gin or brandy as these were cheaper – three and four pesetas against six and eight! On another occasion the boys went on a specially organized outing for young people and were offered Sangria. They returned home somewhat the worse for wear and Jock was not best pleased. They started young!

During the summer holidays I was able to rent two rooms for

Aunty Mary and the boys in adjacent accommodation to the B&B. They would explore locally whilst I was flying and during my free time we were able to visit Eric's relation in the West Country. They were delighted to see us and gave us a wonderful welcome.

The Chief Pilot of Dan-Air, Captain Atkins, came down to Bristol at the beginning of the summer season. He suggested that I should be posted onto the Ambassador up at Newcastle. Although a good step up, I realized that it would be much more difficult to see my family, even though I could commute by air. I refused, saying that I would prefer to remain at Bristol. I couldn't believe it when I was posted to Gatwick on the Ambassador within a week. I was overjoyed! I had been accepted at Bristol and was very grateful, but was glad to be back home though I would miss Captain Faulkener

Naturally, he knew the terrain around Bristol like the back of his hand. When the cloud base was too low for a visual approach and a strong wind required an easterly landing he would descend over the Bristol Channel and approach below the runway level, which was some hundred feet above sea level, before popping up at a certain feature to land safely on same. He also owned his own Dakota which he flew to South America and back and after leaving Dan-Air flew for Malay Airways on Fokker Friendships, before retiring back to the U.K.

....

The Ambassador was a high wing pressurized aircraft, which BEA had called the 'Elizabethan' whilst it was operated extensively on its European routes. It was very popular with passengers as the view from the large windows was not obscured and being pressurized it was often able to fly above some of the weather giving a smoother flight. The aircraft carried forty-nine passengers with plenty of leg room and some tables fixed between rearward and forward facing seats.

The faithful Dakota was not pressurized and could only carry thirty two passengers and climb not above 10,000 feet without oxygen for the passengers, thus having to fly through much of the bad weather.

Two days after being posted I had my first flight on the Ambassador. Supernumery flights were followed by training on the aircraft at Gatwick and then Ostend, which was quieter. My

fellow trainee and I were lucky enough to have Captains Malcolm
Grant and Don Warburton as instructors. They were very good
and forbearing. Flights from Brussels to Malmo and Copenhagen
were also unexpectedly added to the itinerary. Although we were
able to night stop Copenhagen, we sadly arrived too late to see
anything of the city, only catching a glimpse the following
morning on our way back to the airport. Something well known
to aircrew!

Needless to say I also had to study the technical manuals to
take the exams to put the aircraft on my licence.

I only flew on the Ambassador's mainly European flights for
four and a half months before being posted onto a Comet course.
But I have happy memories of the Champagne flights. These were
Licensed Victuallers Charters, which involved taking members to
various vineyards. The crew were always invited to lunch, but
were not supposed to imbibe and instead we were given a bottle
of their Champagne to take home. I will always remember the
beautiful countryside and one really attractive 'Orangerie', a large
separate circular conservatory, in which lunch was served and
which included several delicate dishes, let alone the pink
champagne!

However, the airfields used were small and on one occasion the
taxiway was rather narrow for the wheelbase of the Ambassador.
The passengers were requested to assist the crew in repositioning
the aircraft!

During my short sojourn on the aircraft I was asked to help out
on the Dakota at Bristol for a few days and had to sit up in bed in
the B&B to go through the notes again. I had no idea then that I
would have to do very, very much more studying on the Comet
course, or that it would lead me on to the flying I was to love most.

However, I had learned that one of our Ambassadors, flown by
Captain Larkman, a very senior and experienced pilot, had been
used to determine the cause of the crash of a BEA Ambassador
carrying the victorious Manchester Football team at Munich. It
was found, after prolonged tests at Bedford that slush on the
runway had caused the eventual crash. On the third attempt, the
BEA aircraft had reached a speed greater than that at which it
must become airborne or risk running out of runway. It was
unable to do so and overran the runway crashing into a building,
killing fifteen passengers and injuring many more, including the

manager Sir Matt Busby. The slush had built up a wedge in front of the tyres which eventually separated them from the surface causing the aircraft to aquaplane and prevent effective braking.

During the tests, the slush/water had dramatically sprayed the fuselage and tail plane. The Ambassador wings would also have been impaired by a continuous fall of snow at Munich, which would have built up a rough surface, causing a reduction in lift, a smooth surface being vital. The aircraft had not been de-iced when it returned to the tarmac for an engine inspection after one of the aborted take-offs.

After these tests it became standard procedure for aircraft to be de-iced twenty minutes before take-off and again if this was delayed for any reason and, only a depth of two inches/five centimetres of water or soft snow was permitted for safe take-off or landing. The speed above which aquaplaning could occur was nine times the square root of the tyre pressure, i.e. a car tyre inflated to 25lbs could aquaplane at 45mph. The relevant figure was therefore included in each aircraft's flight manual.

It was due to these tests that, when landing on a wet runway, pilots were advised to 'thump' the aircraft down so that the tyres would penetrate the film of water/slush and make contact with the surface enabling control of direction and efficient braking to be achieved. This was particularly important when there was a crosswind, which could cause the aircraft to slide sideways off the runway. Once, as a passenger myself, I was able to explain this to someone who had complained about the firmness of the touchdown at Palma de Mallorca. It can rain there too!

....

Miguel had written during the year, wanting to come to England, but I had been unable to find him a post in an English hospital. In the meanwhile, he had agreed to help a young man start a restaurant on the coast west of Barcelona. I was able to take some leave late in September and found that an Ambassador flight ended in Manchester, from where a Comet was scheduled to fly to Barcelona. I was granted permission to fly on it supernumery. Unfortunately the beautiful Comet had over an hour's delay due to a malfunctioning instrument. As I had been up early and had already flown to Holland, I did not fully appreciate all the details of this magnificent aircraft. The flight passed in somewhat of a blur as I tried to assimilate the various instruments.

When we finally arrived, Miguel was peering anxiously through the glass of the arrivals area. I was able to surprise him by coming from behind him and tapping him on the shoulder. I had come in via the crew entrance! He was accompanied by his young friend who drove us down the coast to his restaurant. En route we stopped for a meal. I needed the 'Señoras' before proceeding, but didn't initially understand the instructions given in Spanish. Eventually, I found the right entrance, but when trying to leave the cubicle I couldn't open the door. I tried my faithful penknife which I carried, but couldn't move the lock or climb over. I had to resort to putting my head out of the high window and shouting 'Ayuda me' which I hoped was correct for 'help me'. A passerby, hearing my plea, entered the restaurant saying that 'a mad woman in a funny uniform needed 'socorro' – help. One of my most embarrassing moments!

We continued on down the coast to a picturesque old walled town situated on a promontory. The restaurant was in the middle, a large room on the ground floor of a house. Meals were only served of an evening so we had time to explore the town, the bodegas (wine cellars/bars) and the harbour. We were also able to swim from a nearby sandy cove. The cook was an avid fisherman so we regularly had a late lunch at 5pm. I left Barcelona having promised to marry Miguel!

I had never intended to marry again, but his kindness and sincerity had won me over. When I asked my elder son his opinion, he said he wasn't sure, but a month later, having moved up into the senior school, he wrote 'If you are sure, Mother, go ahead'. The younger one, when asked by my step-mother, replied 'He will take the weight off her shoulders.' Step-mother hadn't been too enthusiastic – yet again she thought he wasn't good enough for me! However, she also came to appreciate him. I was very fortunate.

The restaurant in Spain did not prosper so Miguel returned to Menorca and tried to obtain a passport to come to England. However, it took nearly a year due to a rogue official pocketing a required payment after the Spanish Civil War while he was working in northern Spain. He employed two lawyers, but thought that my offer of a third would only complicate things further!

Chapter 17

Dan-Air - Comet

I was suddenly posted onto the Comet 4 fleet at the end of November 1969. The Comet 1 was the very first jet airliner in the world. It had been designed and produced by an inspired team at De Havilland and test flown by their Chief Pilot, John Cunningham, the famous World War Two night-fighter ace.

This beautiful, streamlined and elegant aeroplane had caused a sensation wherever it flew. With its powerful Rolls Royce engines, it could climb twice as high and fly faster than any other airliner – to 40,000 ft and achieve 500 mph. It coped happily with high altitude airfields and did not need any extra runway length.

No wonder my father and all the other passengers loved it because the flight was so smooth and fast. Whilst flying on one of the early BOAC flights he was able to balance a penny coin on its edge on the seat tray throughout the cruise. Despite a series of tragic accidents which occurred two years after the first scheduled passenger flights in 1952, he said he would fly in this magnificent airliner as soon as it was allowed to do so again.

Although De Havilland had conducted more extensive ground tests to a higher standard on the Comet than any other aircraft, they had been unable to duplicate the pressure extremes of continual climbing to and descending from 7 miles high or the extreme temperatures encountered at this altitudes.

Fortunately the Navy recovered enough pieces of the aircraft which crashed into the sea off the coast of Elba for the Royal Aircraft Establishment at Farnborough to discover the effects of hitherto unknown metal fatigue at the corners of the square cabin windows and a hatch in the top of the fuselage, which had been undetectable by the standards of inspection at the time.

Although sadly remembered for this problem, Douglas in America had indeed moved from oval windows in its unpressurized DC4 to the rectangular shape for all their subsequent pressurized developments of the DC6 and DC7. The results had far reaching effects for all future jet aircraft. After the shape of the windows had been changed, the Comet was an incredibly safe aircraft.

....

There were so many innovative systems in the design of the Comet that the technical course lasted four weeks. It was held at the Russ Hill Hotel near Gatwick and conducted by experienced engineers. Unfortunately, one of our instructors went down with a virulent 'flu just before Christmas and I caught it and was prostrate throughout the festivities. I protested that I needed to study, but the doctor was unsympathetic and just said I wouldn't be able to do a thing for a week. He was right. Fortunately Aunty Mary had joined us as usual and, bless her, looked after the boys and cooked the Christmas meal. Sadly I couldn't eat a mouthful. I tried studying on New Year's Eve, but the words went in one eye and out the other! However, I managed to recover in time to take the technical exams and somehow passed.

Next came the simulator training. We had had snow over the previous few days and the roads were still icy. Our not very experienced driver slid all over the place on the way from Gatwick to the simulator centre. I was so nauseous by the time we arrived that I had to stand outside the building in the freezing cold, taking several deep breaths before I dared to go in. However, I then had to concentrate so hard I forgot all about being car sick!

Fortunately the cockpit layout was not completely new to me. On hearing that I might be posted to the Comet, I had requested two more supernumery flights and, during a visit to R.A.F. Lyneham with the British Ninety Nines, had managed to persuade the pilots to allow me to return to do an hour on their Comet simulator. I was very grateful; hands on was very much better than just watching.

During subsequent training sessions we practiced coping with various failures and emergencies. Then, at the beginning

Above: My first official flight as Dakota First Officer for Morton Air Services on 16th January 1965. Below: G-AOUD, one of Morton's Dakotas.

This award was for the best Air Traffic Controller in Europe, the presentation being in Munich, Germany.

The evocative sculpture of hands, defining the guiding and guarding of aircraft safely, I was allowed to keep.

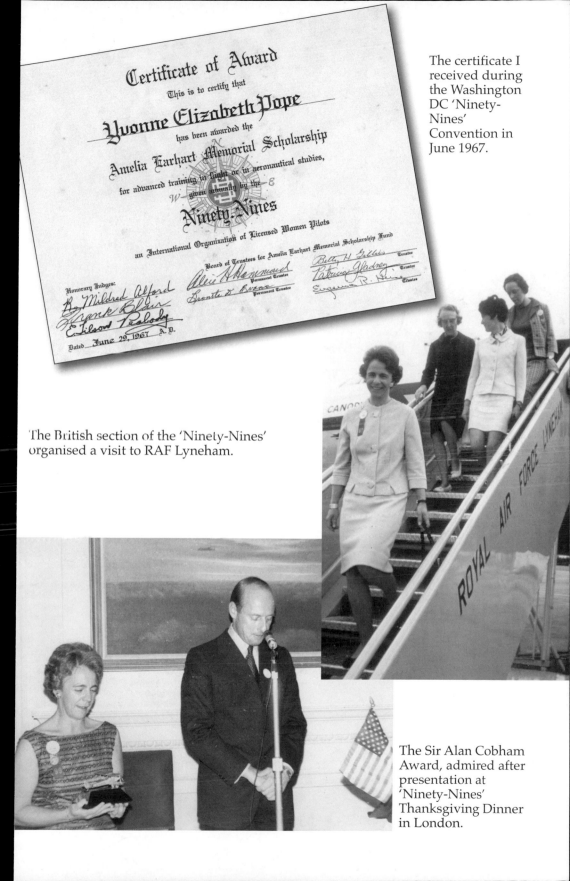

Certificate of Award

This is to certify that

Yvonne Elizabeth Pope

has been awarded the

Amelia Earhart Memorial Scholarship

for advanced training in flight or in aeronautical studies,
given annually by the

Ninety-Nines

an International Organization of Licensed Women Pilots

The certificate I received during the Washington DC 'Ninety-Nines' Convention in June 1967.

The British section of the 'Ninety-Nines' organised a visit to RAF Lyneham.

The Sir Alan Cobham Award, admired after presentation at 'Ninety-Nines' Thanksgiving Dinner in London.

YVONNE POPE British Section	**EVELYN BRAESE** Cape Girardeau Area Chapter	**WENDY BLANCHARD** Washington D.C. Chapter	**ARDYTH TRENHOLM** San Fernando Valley Chapter

Amelia Earhart Memorial Scholarship Winners — 1967

CONGRATLATIONS to WENDY BLANCHARD, EVELYN BRAESE, YVONNE POPE and ARDYTH TRENHOLM — the four Ninety-Nines who were awarded Scholarships of up to $700 each. They were selected from seventy-one applicants and I'm sure that each Ninety-Nine and non - member who has contributed to the Trust in the years since 1941 will be proud to have these women represent our organization.

Actually three of the Scholarships this year have been provided from the Trust and a fourth is the gift of the Michigan SMALL Race Board because—"Our Chapter has benefited so much by the AE Scholarships given within our Chapter (There ha____ three). This is the 30___
AMELIA E____
w____
c____
i____
m____

W____
of a____
child____
rently____
drews____
ington____
Univers____
born a____
dcgree i____
enabling____
methods a____
tor that is____
in flight tra____

hours have been spent in pilot training. Currently holder of ASEL - Commercial - Glider - and Flight Instructor ratings, she will use her Scholarship toward her Instrument and Instrument Instructor ratings.

EVELYN BRAESE and her husband manage a fixed base operation in Dyersburg, Tennessee, which they took over in 1962 when it was about to gasp its last breath. At the present time, they rank 12th in the state in terms of traffic movements. This, they have accomplished almost single handedly while raising three boys. Immediately

____, presents
____ an Amelia Earhart
____rship to **DEEDO HEISE** and
ALICE HAMMOND, Trustees of the
Fund.

upon taking over the airport, EVELYN became her husband's first student on the field and when not taking care of her family and handling the business details of the operation, has managed to acquire Commercial, Single and Multi-engine Land and Ground Instructor ratings. She is currently teaching the ground school courses, helping train the 65 pilots they have graduated, and flying Charter. She will apply her Scholarship toward an Instrument rating in order to fly night charter and under instrument conditions.

YVONNE ELIZABETH POPE of Lambs Crescent, England is a widow with two sons 9 and 11. She is currently employed as first officer on Heron and Dakota aircraft and Captain on Doves for Morton Air Service LTD. and associate of British United Airways, and is one of the very few women flying for a commercial airline. Born in Pretoria, South Africa and educated in both England and South Africa, YVONNE learned to fly between trips as an airline hostess, and was eventually accepted by the Women's Royal Air Force Volunteer Reserve. She was the first woman to be accepted by the British Ministry of Aviation for Training as an Air Controller and while assigned to Gatwick airport (London) was awarded the 1965 Air Traffic Controllers Award of all Europe. YVONNE currently is holder of British Private and Commercial Pilot Licenses, Instrument rating, full

July-August, ____

— 7 —

Above: A surprise 'Ninety-Nines' Amelia Earhart Scholarship Award helped to obtain the British Airline Transport Licence. The visit to America culminating in a visit to the Kennedy Space Center.

Opposite page: Looking to the skies and very honoured by a true Trail Blazer.

SR ALAN J. COBHAM, K.B.E., A.F.C., Hon.F.R.Ae.S.

Telephone: WIMBORNE 2121

LEIGH PARK,
WIMBORNE,
DORSET.

3rd July, 1968.

Mrs. Y. Pope,
Skyway,
9 Lambs Crescent,
Horsham, Sussex.

Thank you so much for your letter of
the 26th June.

I was delighted to hear that you have
now obtained your Airline Transport Pilots'
Licence.   A thousand congratulations - carry
on the good work.   I am quite sure you will
get to the top very shortly.

Kindest regards,

Yours truly,
Alan J Cobham

Truly a beauty of the skies. (Kurt Lang)

So happy to be going to fly the Comet I loved!

Dear Madam, I may be a "chauvanistic pig" but I take my hat off to the most skilfull pilot I've ever flown with. Yours. Charlie.

P.S. This is my first flight!!

I should not have done the PA talk to the passengers - or just after one of my good landings!

How lucky I am to be in the Comet cockpit.

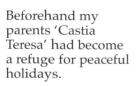

Above: a happy second
marriage in Menorca
22nd October 1970.

Above and left: the
gardeners stone
cottage/shed in Alcaufar
which became our
retirement 'Perlita', little
pearl, which grew and
grew.

Beforehand my
parents 'Castia
Teresa' had become
a refuge for peaceful
holidays.

Memorandum

DAN-AIR SERVICES LTD.

TO: F/O Mrs. Sintes

FROM: Chief Pilot

21st March, 1972

This is to confirm your promotion to A.748 Captain, with effect from the 17th March, 1972.

Please accept my congratulations on obtaining this position.

Captain R.E. Atkins
Chief Pilot.

My first airline command - the Avro 748. The date? 21st March 1972.

Memorandum

DAS 20

DAN-AIR SERVICES LTD.

TO: Captain Sintes.

FROM: Captain P. Hall
Comet Fleet Manager.

DATE: 21st March, 1972.

Dear Yvonne,

I have just learned that you are now the boss of your own 748. Many congratulations - I am delighted and look forward to the day when you will graduate to one of our bigger jobs.

Sincerely,

Captain P. Hall

Above: Whitney Straight,(standing) addressing HRH Princess Anne (far left) and the President of the Royal Aeronautical Society after the presentation of his amazing award to me by Princess Anne.

The Whitney Straight Award

PRESENTED BY

Her Royal Highness The Princess Anne
Mrs Mark Phillips

ON MONDAY 20 MAY 1974
AT 17.30 TO

Mrs Yvonne Sintes

AT THE ROYAL
AERONAUTICAL SOCIETY
4 HAMILTON PLACE
LONDON W1

Left: In the cockpit of a BAC 1-11, my first jet command in 1975. It was kind of my ATC colleageues to congratulate me!

Below: G-AZED, one of Dan-Air's fleet of 1-11s.

I was glad that Dan-Air's
normal service was
appreciated.

The National Farmers' Union

Devon County Branch
Honiton & Axminster Branches
N.F.U. Office, High Street, Honiton, Devon.
Telephone: Honiton 2051

County Secretary
R.H. CROWLE, B.Sc.

Group Secretary
A.E. CLARKE, ACIS.

Our Ref:
AEC/BH

Your Ref:

19th May, 1976.

Captain Sinters,
C/o Dan Air Services Ltd.,
Bilbao House,
36-38 New Broad Street,
LONDON. E.C.2.

Dear Captain Sinters,

Inghams Charter Flight DA1837 from
Athens to Gatwick on 3rd May, 1976.

I apologise for the delay in this long overdue note of appreciation for
the extraordinary courtesy which you and your Crew extended to us on the above
occasion when our flight was delayed some four hours at Athens air-port.

As an Aircraft Captain, your skill and leadership go without saying and
it was very evident from the cheerful and willing spirit of your Staff that you
command a very happy ship and I feel priviledged to have flown with you. You
were also infinitely patient with all the many people you allowed on the flight
deck and certainly could not have done more to offset our frustration caused by
events completely beyond your control.

All good wishes for the future,

Yours sincerely,

A.E. Clarke
Group Secretary.

Receiving the British Air Line
Pilot's Silver Medal for
contributions to air Safety,
delivered and positioned by the
Dan-Air Captain.

After delivery via Dan -Air
1-11 to Menorca.

Celebrating with a huge 'ensaimada' pastry cake, after last landing in Menorca before retiring. The hidden Champagne was only imbibed on return to Gatwick!

Yvonne and Miguel before a special Dan-Air dinner.

Ensaimada was happily given by Miguel's family, nieces Sabina, Teresa and nephew young Miguel.

Perlita patio garden after a few years of retirement.

My sister Toni with her cats in South Africa - we had plenty in Menorca.

Miguel's 80th birthday party with his brother Juan and dear wife Catalina

My sister Marcelle with son Nick and husband Unal, all living in Australia.

Miguel with Liz and Chris on holiday

Again on holiday, a happy lunch with Samantha, Barbara Jon and Lewis.

At the Dan-Air Staff Association lunch in May 2013 celebrating 60 years of the airline starting operations and 20 years since the association was founded to keep the spirit of Dan-Air going.

Granny Yvonne with great grandson 'Monty' - perhaps the next airline pilot / astronaut!?

of February 1970, came the really exciting part – the actual flying of the aircraft. Familiarization started en route from Gatwick to Teeside, previously the R.A.F. aerodrome known as Middleton St George. I was the last in line of the trainees and to my amazement was talked down on the approach and allowed to do the landing! We stayed at the hotel on the airport which had been developed from the Officers Mess. It was said that it was haunted by an R.A.F. Vampire pilot who had crashed into it and was unable to pass on. People based there said they had seen him but were unable to help. Time, fortunately, eventually released him.

Thank goodness the only incident that involved a Comet during training occurred years later when someone on a check flight landed wheels-up. The landing was so smooth that the Captain only noticed it because the landing run was shorter than usual!

Even though it was early February, the weather on the whole was kind to us. I was able to fly eight days out of ten, practising handling the aircraft in normal and emergency situations, including landing with and without flaps and with simulated engine failures. The instructors were very good and I found the training exhilarating. Whilst awaiting my turn I would stand outside the terminal building watching this wonderful aeroplane thinking 'do I really fly her?'! She climbed like a 'home-sick angel' and I didn't want her to stop. She flew like a dream and was amazingly flexible in descent.

There was so much power available from the four Rolls Royce Avon engines embedded in the wings that one could only tell if one had failed from the instruments. There were no physical symptoms and she would fly happily on three. Indeed there was an idea put forward to do so whilst at cruising altitude to save on fuel. The ministry did not approve! Her big flaps were a special design feature which enabled this clean, streamlined aircraft to slow down very easily from a fast approach speed to the landing one, the last selection giving the braking effect of huge 'barn doors'.

It was great having a Flight Engineer as part of the crew. He looked after all the different systems, including transfer of fuel from one tank to another in the huge wings and any de-icing if required. One of the engineers, big Jock Mills, had kindly tried to teach me something about the various systems on a supernumery flight, but his Scottish accent was so strong that I wasn't able to catch all of it!

During training all the pilots were checked to the standard required of a Captain, so that if he became ill the second pilot could take over. Having finished at Teeside , we started three months supervised route flying to prove that we could cope with all that was required before sharing the actual hands-on flying.

My first route flight was on the 14th February to Las Palmas and took 4 hours 23 minutes. The normal procedure was for the pilot not flying the aeroplane to do the R.T. With the faster speed of the Comet the setting up of the radio aids and position reporting came somewhat rapidly. It wasn't until we were on the long sector from Lisbon to the Canary Islands that I really appreciated that we were serenely flying over the Atlantic at 35,000 ft! However, I also learned how intermittent the long distance H.F. (high frequency) radio contact could be. It required patience and persistence.

During route training I flew to several different and interesting destinations, including Venice, Berlin, Tenerife, Malaga, Faro, Alicante, Tunis and Pula on the tip of the Yugoslav Peninsular. I was really great when we didn't have to restrict our climb after take-off and could soar upwards. Unfortunately, due to noise restrictions at busy airports, aircraft usually had to reduce power and be restricted in height whilst following sometimes complex departure routes, avoiding built up areas and inbound traffic. I always felt it was degrading to curb our superb aircraft's ascent and resented it every time!

In between route training I was due some leave so took it over Easter. Jock Betty and Andrew were once again able to join us in Menorca. Betty was very proud of the fact that she had learned to swim during the winter and desperately wanted to show off her new prowess in the sea. I knew it would be far too cold, but couldn't let her go in on her own. I think we were in the water for exactly one minute before we came out gasping for two double brandies! Sadly Miguel's lawyers had not managed to advance very far towards obtaining his passport, so he was not able to return to England with us.

....

Returning to Comet flying helped. However, on one occasion as we relaxed in the cockpit at Gatwick after a route flight, a senior training Captain came on board to take over and stood talking to us. Unknown to us, he quietly pressed a test button for a fire alarm. Half out of the cockpit we fell back into our seats, not really knowing whether to believe, but thinking we should do something about it. He just said it could have been for real. We weren't sure whether to forgive him!

Towards the end of my route training I had a nightmare in which the Captain collapsed and I hadn't done a landing since completing my initial training at Teeside. Fortunately my next flight was with Keith Moody, another training captain who understood and let me 'save his life'. I soon learned that there was a great camaraderie in Dan-Air.

On one occasion, three Dan-Air Comets participated in the Dutch Bulb flights, transporting people who wanted to see the beauty of the massed bulbs in full bloom. We all night-stopped in an over-full hotel in Rotterdam. I would not have believed it possible that all three crews could somehow fit into a small single bedroom to enjoy an evening drink together. A crew comprised two pilots, an engineer and four hostesses.

One crew sat on the floor side by side, backs to the wall, another crew did the same on the opposite side, with the third crew on the bed and any chair available! Needless to say we only caught a glimpse of the bulbs on our way back to the airport for an onward flight to Berlin, which was an experience in itself.

The aircraft was only safe within one of the corridors fanning out on the western side of the city. They crossed Russian occupied German territory. Maintaining an exact heading and height were vital.

Once fully checked out as a First Officer, I flew farther afield to many places I had not seen before (mostly airports!). These included Corfu, Athens, Rhodes, Nicosia in Cyprus, Istanbul and Izmir in Turkey and Dubai in the Arab Emirates. I will never forget the beautiful view from miles high of the islands of Crete and Rhodes set in the blue of the Mediterranean Sea.

Very sadly, one of our Comets crashed near Barcelona,

having been cleared to descend to a height that was too low for the surrounding mountains. I sent a telegram to Miguel to reassure him that I was safe. Unfortunately it was delivered to another Miguel Sintes who happened to be in the village and he wondered what on earth it was all about. I learned the reason why the mother's surname is always added to the father's in Spain, for example, Miguel Sintes Marti, not just Miguel Sintes!

In between my Comet flying I was asked if I would act as a Safety Instrument Pilot for April and James Clavell.

They had learned to fly in America but were humble about their qualifications, realizing they didn't have enough experience to be happy in poor weather conditions. Initially I flew locally with April and was impressed by her thorough pre-flight check and competence in the air. They owned a Cessna 337 which could carry four passengers. Then over a weekend, April and I flew to Menorca via Perpignan. It was strange to be flying so slowly again in a small aircraft!

As it was arranged at the last minute, I was unable to warn Miguel and we walked in on him whilst he was helping a pleasant English lady with her bar/restaurant. April and I stayed in the pension (B&B) in Alcaufar overnight, flying back the next day via Beauvais. She was so good, I didn't touch the controls.

James Clavell had been a Japanese prisoner of war and had afterwards become the famous author of several novels beginning with King Rat and continuing with Shogun, etc. He started by writing film scripts and went on to direct and produce. April had supported him throughout, initially becoming a model to do so. She was very elegant, attractive, artistic and capable as well as being a thoroughly nice person.

Three weeks later, James was able to co-incide with me on days off and we again flew to Menorca. This time they were able to take their two daughters with them and hired a car to see something of the island. April flew the aircraft down there and James was most surprised when I allowed him to do all the flying back to the U.K. Other safety pilots had taken over if the weather had deteriorated at all. We had to request a change of level due to icing, but there were no other problems.

At their home in London, I was bemused to meet Michael

Caine, his beautiful wife Shakira, and Omar Sharif, when they were involved in the making of 'The Last Valley'.

April and James became members of the Ninety Nines, James having to be a reluctant 'Sixty Six' as husband. By so doing he was supposed (tongue in cheek) to support, assist and be subservient to his Ninety Nine wife in anything to do with flying - and yet he was the man who wrote the script for the film '633 Squadron'!

....

Dan-Air was chartered to fly Berliners to many favourite holiday destinations in Spain, Italy, Yugoslavia and North Africa. My first week entailed flying to Palma, Rimini and Dubrovnik. During time off between flights, we explored some of the city of Berlin. I was impressed by the wide tree-lined avenues and the ease with which one could get out of the centre into the green wooded countryside – 'Grunewald' – and take a trip on the river. It was, however, sad and depressing to see the 'Wall' being built, dividing East and West Germany, the actual boundary being in the centre of the river. The grey police boats patrolling the drab eastern side of the river were in great contrast to the pleasure steamers and working barges plying the western half with its little enclaves of sandy beaches filled with cheerful families.

Shortly afterwards I was rostered to do an R.A.F. charter with Captain Atkins, our Chief Pilot. I had not flown with him before so was somewhat in awe. After take-off, the undercarriage wouldn't come up. We went to Mayfield, Gatwick's holding beacon, to sort the problem out. Having done so, we set off again.

To lighten things, I asked if he was glad he had left his office that morning. I don't think he appreciated it! However, all went well thereafter and we landed at Akrotiri in Cyprus five hours and eleven minutes later.

As there were no passengers for the return flight I was allowed to fly the aircraft. Coming up towards Athens, Air Traffic suddenly advised me that our Company wished us to divert to 'Gili'. Captain 'Atkins was in the cabin at the time. Having only heard of the opera singer by that name, I had to ask for the four letter code. It turned out to be Izmir. One of our

Comets had gone 'sick' (developed a fault) so that it couldn't return to the U.K. with passengers on board. Knowing that we were returning empty, the Captain had requested our diversion. On arrival, we had no trouble in being given permission to land, but when the passengers had been transferred and we requested start-up clearance, it was denied. We were told the authorities concerned had not yet given us permission to land! Our poor passengers had to wait yet another hour. As our duty day would exceed fifteen hours, Captain 'Atkins had to ask the crew if they were prepared to continue. We all naturally said 'yes'. We had taken off at 08.10 and finally landed back at Gatwick at 23.25. We definitely enjoyed a drink on arrival! It had been a worthwhile day.

As the Comets were used mainly on Inclusive Tour Charters, the summer was a very busy one. As well as flying out of Gatwick, we flew from Glasgow and Edinburgh in Scotland, Manchester and Liverpool in the midlands, and Berlin, being based away from home for up to five days at a time.

Whilst in Glasgow I met up with the daughter of my father's friend, whom I admired greatly. As a slight attractive blonde, she had driven huge articulated long-loaders up and down the country during World War II, transporting damaged aircraft and aircraft parts. The incredible work done by women in both wars is easily forgotten. As well as working in an arms factory, Eric's mother drove a tram in World War I!

In between flying from Manchester, I was able to spend a few evenings with the wife of an Air Traffic Controller. She had been very kind to me during my time with Mortons and it was good to be able to catch up with her. Even if one doesn't see the world and becomes tired of hotel bedrooms, details away from home can be rewarding.

....

As summer leave was at a premium, it was allocated every second year, according to a rota. I had only recently joined the Comet fleet so was not eligible that first year. Jock wasn't able to take leave either so I asked a pleasant motherly friend from Air Traffic Control if she would accompany Jon and Chris to Menorca. The holiday went reasonably well, but I was told that she was very strict.

I was able to take some leave towards the end of October, shortly after a ferry flight from Berlin back to Gatwick with Captain Arthur Larkman, who was born in Australia and had initially flown for Malaya Airways for seven years, mainly on Dakotas. The flight was really pleasant and surprisingly uneventful despite returning on three engines, the fourth engine having failed, demonstrating again the amazing adaptability of the Comet.

In 1956 he had decided on a move. Whilst on holiday in England he met up with an old friend who had become Chief Pilot of Dan-Air. He was persuaded to join the Company and see something of Europe. In order to do so he found he had to be examined in British Air Law and sit a technical exam on the Dakota, despite having flown over 6,000 hours on the aircraft! He also had to undergo the Instrument Rating Flying Test.

He went on to fly most of the different aircraft the Company bought over the years. As well as conducting the slush trials on the Ambassador, he flew the Black Knight Rockets to Woomera in Australia when Dan-Air was chartered by the Ministry of Defence. Black Knight was to prove very important to the development of rocket technology. The heat shield developed by British scientists was vital to the recovery of the instrumentation and together with many other advances, was adopted by the Americans. Britain sadly gained little from her ingenuity as the Government withdrew its funding.

Arthur became Chief Training Captain and in between a full personal flying programme, organised all the training on the various aircraft, doing much of it himself. As well as being Deputy Chief Pilot, he eventually joined the Board as Director of Operations, bringing his commonsense to bear on any problem. He was great to fly with, giving his co-pilots so much confidence in themselves. He was also instrumental in the Company employing two part-time women pilots, Beryl Sanders and Claire Roberts, while I was flying for Mortons. Unfortunately, part-time flying was discontinued by the Ministry.

His attractive and dynamic wife, Joy, saw little of him during his flying and training sessions, but in between, aided and abetted him. They both tried in vain to discourage their son and daughter from having anything to do with aviation, but their son, Brod, became a pilot and daughter Sue an hostess with the company. Little did I think that Brod would fly with me as a First Officer when I became Captain.

As I did not want Dan-Air to think that I would wish to give up flying, I did not mention that I was going to use my October leave to re-marry. I asked Freddie Laker for the tickets to and from Menorca and was even prepared to sit on the steps of the Passport Office until they gave Miguel his passport. Fortunately, it was issued just before I arrived! Nan was kind enough to give us her blessing and the use of Casita Teresa for our honeymoon.

As my family could not attend, we decided to marry very quietly in the little chapel in Alcaufar with just two witnesses. We asked the daughter of the lady Miguel had helped whilst starting her restaurant, and a local taxi driver. There was a thunderstorm the night before our day and the little chapel was flooded. The Priest and the taxi driver had to borrow mops and buckets from the Pension before the ceremony could take place. On arrival we found there was an extra witness, the daughter's boyfriend, perhaps to give him the right idea! In the middle of the service there was the sound of children's feet. An Irish lady called Judy, with a holiday home in the village, her two boys and au pair joined us. They had been advised by the local postman!

Fortunately, the service was conducted in Spanish, not Menorcean, so I understood most of it. Miguel was so emotional at the end that Irish Judy had to tap him on the shoulder and say 'Kiss her!' Afterwards we took everyone to the Pension/Bar, Via Maris, where we gave the children ice-creams and the grown-ups Champagne. Having booked lunch in the Hotel Xuroy, we slipped away quietly, leaving them to enjoy themselves. We gather they did!

We had not told Miguel's family anything, intending to surprise them, but were beaten to it by the airport reporter. He had heard a rumour and had been following us up and down the Island as we sorted out the paper-work. We hadn't kept our promise of telling him when, so he retaliated with an article in the local paper the next day, saying that both families had attended a large celebration! Not having seen the paper, we phoned Miguel's brother with the glad tidings, only to be told

'Yes, I know'! We spent the next week placating all the many relations, but his brother Juan, very simpatica wife Catalina, and the family forgave us and invited us to a lovely family meal. We were able to spend the last few days quietly sitting by the creek in Alcaufar enjoying the autumn sunshine.

However, when we came to check in for our flight back to England, we found that it had already departed. Freddie Laker's Commercial Manager had been so tired at the end of the season that he had put the wrong departure time on our tickets – and it was the last direct flight! The inter-island flights were fully booked for the next two days so we had a little extra time on our Island. We managed to get on the first flight to Palma the following Monday morning, but had to spend the rest of that day and half the night on the airport, due to restrictions on aircraft landing at Gatwick between midnight and 6 am. Miguel learned the hard way what it was like to fly sub-load staff travel!

However, things worked out surprisingly well as southern England had been lashed by heavy rain all over the weekend and the vicious front cleared Gatwick whilst we were on final approach, so Miguel's first sight of England was in bright sunlight on Tuesday 5th November 1970.

Aunty Mary, Jon and Chris greeted us on our arrival home. Surprisingly, Aunty took to Miguel immediately. Initially she hadn't thought me good enough to marry her nephew, Eric, and I had been concerned that she would not approve. She even gave me a pretty feminine present! However, everyone liked Miguel, he was so simpatico and kind and had an engaging sense of humour. He found several jobs to start with until he was finally able to work with disadvantaged children in a nearby hospital. He also introduced several Spanish dishes to the family menu and taught us the New Year's Eve custom of consuming a grape for every stroke of Big Ben!

I didn't tell Dan-Air that I had re-married as I didn't want them to think that I would give up flying. However, an observant hostess noticed the two wedding rings on my left hand and I was called into the Chief Pilot's office. Captain Atkins said it was the best news he had had that day and suggested that I change my surname to simplify the paper work. So I became Yvonne Sintes in the U.K., but would officially be known as Yvonne van den Hoek Kyle in Spain – father and mother's surnames being used. A wife did not take her husband's name in Spain!

....

Our Comets were fairly busy that winter. Just before Christmas we flew to Venice for the day. Arriving early we changed into civilian clothes in the hotel and then started exploring by taking a boat to St Mark's Square where we seemed to be the only people wandering across it. The air was crisp and clear and we couldn't believe that we had the famous square almost to ourselves.

We then decided to explore the narrow streets leading off the Square in order to find somewhere to eat. After eating, we decided we could walk back to the hotel, but became lost in the labyrinth. Finding a street heading back to water, we gratefully boarded a boat, but it called in at every stop en route and after nearly biting our finger nails with anxiety, we only reached our hotel in time for a very quick change back into uniform. It was a unique experience!

Christmas that year was a very happy one with Aunty Mary again joining us. On Boxing Day we visited Nan and her two sisters.

We were able to have a good family holiday in Menorca the next Easter, but on our return found a message saying that my mother had been killed by two youngsters speeding on an inside lane. Sudden death is always more of a shock to overcome than an expected one due to illness. Flying helped, but it took a while.

Fortunately the Comets were kept pretty busy flying to all the tourist destinations. Flying over the Tirol and Dolomite mountains was truly beautiful and gave an insight to the next life. Flying over lovely countryside, above or in between snow-capped mountains, is always incredibly emotive. Even distant views can be majestic and help with healing.

I didn't mind being called out on a day off if Miguel was working. On one occasion it was only to position an aircraft to Shannon for the onward crew to take it across the Atlantic. Only a few of us were checked out on that route. You could be fined by American Air Traffic if you misunderstood their clearance procedure!

On another occasion I was called out to go to three different destinations in the space of fifteen minutes, ending up with a flight to Dubai. I didn't have any summer clothing to hand so had to make do and buy a swimsuit and kaftan in a market near the hotel during our two day wait for the returning aircraft. I soon learned why the kaftan is so comfortable in the heat!

Nearing London on our way back, an American pilot, hearing my voice, broke RT discipline with 'Say honey, do you really fly that thing?' Fortunately I was flying with the Captain who had checked me out on the Ambassadors. Malcolm Grant answered for me!

We also had a day charter to Paris. Landing at Beauvais, the passengers, followed by ourselves, were transported by coaches to the centre of the city. We set off in search of the famous River Seine. I eventually had to ask a gendarme directing traffic in the middle of a busy thoroughfare, 'Ou est la Seine?' 'La bas' he condescendingly replied to the mad English tourist – and there it was, just below the next block! We found a bar/café for lunch and explored on our way back to the coach pick-up area. Our transport was delayed so the passengers arrived at Beauvais ahead of us. There was no time to change into uniform so I had to fly the Comet back in my smart black and white dress and court shoes!

Apart from the death of my mother, 1971 was a really good year. The home scene was happy and tranquil and the flying very rewarding. With Miguel's help we started a vegetable garden and herbaceous border.

I even enjoyed doing some weeding and getting my hands into the earth after a day in the sky. In between flying I was able to show Miguel something of the beautiful English countryside. We were invited down to stay with friends in Dartmouth, Devon. The husband was a civil engineer attached to the Naval College so we were able to have a close-up view of the impressive buildings in their well kept grounds. We also managed a boat trip up and down the River Dart and an English tea with scones and cream on the way home.

I also flew to places I had not yet been – Zaragoza, Rome, Naples, Ibiza, Bucharest, Constanta, Frankfurt, Zurich, Barcelona, Gerona, Helsinki and Stockholm. I even flew to

Mahon in Menorca once! At one time, whilst I was holding off over the runway before touching down at Barcelona, a sudden sharp rain shower occurred and it felt as if the Comet had landed itself because my vision was impaired. It was also really beautiful to see the Bay of Naples on a clear day, and funny to at last see the snow covered runway at Stockholm delineated by soft little fir trees.

I felt really privileged when I was able to escape a gloomy day on the ground by climbing through the grey clouds up into the bright sunlight above and look down on the shimmering carpet of white cloud tops far below.

At the end of 1971 I learned that I was not going to escape to that bright sunlight quite so easily. I was offered a captaincy on the Avro 748. I had flown one thousand and thirty two hours on the Comet and was grateful for every minute.

Chapter 18

First Command - H.S. 748

The conversion course for the Avro 748 started in January 1972 and was undertaken by the manufacturers based at Woodford in the Midlands. A.V. Roe had designed the 748 aircraft in 1957 as yet another Dakota replacement but the manufacturing company was taken over in 1963 by Hawker Siddeley. It was a twin engine turbo-propeller aircraft intended mainly for short haul services and carried forty nine passengers.

We were introduced to it in a large hangar before the start of the classroom course, after which it was back to the old routine of sitting up in bed studying after the evening meal. Thank goodness the hotel was warm!

Having passed the Air Registration Board technical exam, I was posted up to Newcastle for the flying training early in February. In between and during the ground course and flying, I was happily able to slip home to see Miguel and the boys, if they had an outing from school. Fortunately my best friend's sister, Mary Rowe, lived in the city with her husband and they kindly offered to put me up and save me staying in yet another hotel. They were very good to me, always giving me a warm welcome no matter what time I returned. Her husband, Brian, had been in the Army so they understood.

The weather during February was very gloomy but the familiarization flying was completed quite quickly. However, the route training encountered snow and heavy rain. Although I didn't see much of the sun, it was good for instrument flying!

Our working day usually consisted of many sectors. I initially flew supernumery to Manchester, Bristol, Cardiff, Liverpool and return. Route checks then followed including Amsterdam and Glasgow, involving five to six sectors a day with turnaround times varying from five to thirty minutes at the most. After a final route check with Captain John Ryder, I was let loose in SOLE COMMAND on the unsuspecting public on the 20th March 1972. We flew from Leeds to Glasgow, back to Leeds then Liverpool/Amsterdam/Liverpool and finally to Leeds again. Total flying time 7 hours 25 minutes, and six landings.

For the next four days I flew from Leeds to Glasgow and Back to Leeds each day, but on the 3rd April extended the day by flying Liverpool/Amsterdam/Liverpool/ Jersey/Gatwick/Luton, and on the 4th April I was able to fly the second half of the inaugural flight for the new weekday Link City Service. This service started from Luton at 0800 local time, calling at Leeds en route to Glasgow and then back to Leeds and vice versa of an evening, scheduled to return to Luton at 2130.

Passenger reaction was varied. The cabin crew always enjoyed watching their faces when they heard my voice. I think the men were reasonably pragmatic on the whole, probably thinking that it must be alright if the Company allowed me to be in the cockpit. The ladies initially seemed more dubious, thinking perhaps that only men flew aeroplanes, when in fact women in the Air Transport Auxiliary, A.T.A., flew all types of aircraft from the small Tiger Moth to the biggest bombers during the Second World War. These wonderful women delivered them to where they were required, often in poor weather conditions without any of the aids available to modern pilots. Sadly they were forgotten after hostilities ceased.

On one occasion, after we had landed at Glasgow, some French tourists who had heard my voice en route and couldn't believe it, had to walk round to the front of the aircraft to see for themselves. However, some months later when I went into the cabin to explain a problem, a lady passenger sitting in a front seat said 'Oh, I am glad we have a woman pilot!'

....

Having learned that I was to be based at Luton I tried to find accommodation and work for Miguel there, but without success, so I decided to commute. I preferred not to hurry in the mornings and give myself time for a cooked breakfast. It meant getting up at 3am to leave the house by 5am in order to allow plenty of time to reach Luton by seven o'clock. I then wouldn't normally return home until around midnight. Fortunately, the late return was followed by a minimum of twelve hours rest, and the programme was varied. Sometimes I had three early mornings a week, flying Monday, Wednesday and Friday from Luton to Leeds/Glasgow/Leeds, where we had a rest in a hotel before finishing the evening schedule by flying back to Luton. On other days I flew Luton/Leeds/Glasgow/Leeds to night stop, and would then take the aircraft the following day to Liverpool for the Amsterdam Service, returning via Liverpool to Leeds to do the first part of the evening Link Service, which was from Leeds to Glasgow and back to Leeds. After night stopping again at Leeds, I would complete the Link schedule the next evening, Leeds/Glasgow/Leeds and back to Luton.

Complex? Take a breath and start again! I have had to do so whilst consulting my log book. I didn't envy the people who did the rostering! Over some weekends we would have to position the aircraft from Luton to Gatwick early on a Saturday morning to fly to Jersey and back. Other times we would fly Gatwick/Jersey/Gatwick/ Ostend/Gatwick. On the Sunday we could fly Gatwick/Jersey/Brussels/Jersey/ Gatwick, taking off at 0855 to return at 1955. On other occasions it was just to Jersey and back and then position the aircraft to Luton, arriving there past midnight.

I did have some weekends free to catch up with my family and, as Miguel's work with disadvantaged children in a nearby hospital involved variable hours, we also had a few midweek days off together. Whenever I had an early start I would try not to disturb him and likewise when I arrived home in the early hours, he would do his best not to wake me when he had to be up at 6am. It must have been difficult for him to adjust to my life, but he accepted it without complaining. I appreciated it greatly. Having been a paramedic during the Spanish Civil War, he had coped with so many difficult hours and problems and had seen so much.

....

Once again weather was an important factor in time keeping as far as the schedules were concerned. Both Leeds and Luton could, on occasions, have fog problems at inappropriate times, Leeds at around 9am and Luton at 9.30pm. We would have to make an approach and, if nothing was seen at the safe break-off height, climb up and perhaps try a second time.

If unsuccessful, we could enter the airfield's holding pattern hoping for a forecast improvement or divert to an alternative airfield immediately. Foggy conditions are very variable and a weather clearance sufficient for landing somewhat unpredictable. We were allowed to start an approach if the reported runway visibility was 600 metres or more. The safety break-off height was usually 200 feet for an approach using the Instrument Landing system, but higher if only a radio beacon was used as it did not give such accurate guidance. If a Precision Approach Radar talk down by an Air Traffic Controller was available this could be used right down to the ground if necessary, similar to the auto land system which later came into use, but these were only available at the larger airports. A surveillance radar approach was not quite as accurate so the safety break-off height was higher, and if the ground, or lights, were not seen at that height, we could have to divert.

It wasn't until I became a Captain that I realised that several people were still afraid of flying. I learned that it was important to inform passengers what was happening when I was a passenger myself on a return flight to Luton. I had checked the weather for the Captain and it was supposed to be good, but weather being a law unto itself and Luton being unpredictable, fog had materialised. We made an approach but then suddenly the power went on and we were climbing up. Without anything being said, another approach was made, but nothing was seen. As we climbed up again, I hoped we would divert. One is told that concentration can deteriorate during a third attempt. Fortunately the Captain then advised us that we would go to East Midlands and await a clearance.

No sooner were we on the ground there than Luton did its usual trick – the visibility improved and we were able to return. After that I always tried to tell the passengers what was happening. If the weather was forecast to be marginal, I would advise them in advance of our intentions, saying that if we couldn't see the ground at our safe height we would climb up and sort out our options so that hopefully they wouldn't be too concerned if they heard the power being applied.

I was lucky on the whole and only twice had to make two approaches at Leeds and then hold for a while. Luton could suddenly become very misty, but fortunately remained above limits for me.

After a lady on an Amsterdam flight told me that she liked the 748 because she only felt safe when she could see the wheels go down, I asked the stewardesses if they saw anyone who seemed nervous to invite them up to the cockpit, if there was time. I would then try to show them simply what we did, pointing out the main instruments and telling them we knew what all the others should read. Unfortunately we can't help in this way anymore as the cockpit is locked against terrorists.

However, there was one person I would never again have invited up to my cockpit. He was a well known journalist who interviewed me for a television programme on women in so-called men's jobs. He asked intelligent questions on the ground but, during a busy sector in the air whilst I was monitoring a new young co-pilot, asked 'What happens at a certain time of the month?' I replied, 'What happens when a brain surgeon has a blazing row with his wife before he leaves home?!' At the first stop I told him how disappointed and disgusted I was with him. To give him his due he did apologise and didn't use that offending part of the footage.

Early on, after any exposure to the media, I would receive some abusive phone calls, a few being only hoarse breathing. On one occasion my younger son happened to be visiting, so he breathed heavily back and that put paid to them! Having been accepted as a flying instructor and an Air Traffic Controller the calls came as a bit of a shock. I later discovered that other women pilots suffered from these calls too and suggested that they also breathed back! I began to realise that these sad calls came from unhappy, dissatisfied people.

Fortunately, as an antidote, flying over the UK countryside was beautiful, when we could see it, the Lake District in particular. I hate to admit that I have only seen it from the air! However the Avro 748 was not, alas, like the Comet. It was no 'homesick angel'. With a full load on a warm day I wondered if it climbed as well as the dear old Dakota. It would also take a long time to climb through icing cloud. One day en route to Amsterdam the ice build up on the wings was so heavy that I had to descend below cloud to get rid of it and maintain level flight. After landing at Amsterdam I came into the cabin before all the Women's Institute passengers had disembarked and was greeted by one of the ladies saying how good it was to have an all female crew. At that moment, of all moments, my First Officer – male - stepped out of the cockpit! Nevertheless, Dan-Air was the first airline in the UK to have an all female crew two years later.

On another occasion I was asked to rescue some football passengers who had been stranded in Jersey over a weekend due to fog. I managed to land during a brief weather improvement. The passengers had been waiting in the terminal for some time and were 'quite happy'. After boarding the aircraft a slightly concerned stewardess reported that they were in no hurry to sit down. Having read all the W.E. John's Biggles aviation adventure books from school days onwards, I rather enjoyed saying 'This is Captain Mrs Bigglesworth, I am afraid the weather is deteriorating rapidly again and if you don't sit down in the nearest seat you will be stuck in Jersey for another day or two'. They were so shocked by the female voice that they did so immediately!

A very unusual incident occurred in January 1973. Whilst day stopping in Leeds I received a phone call from the 748 Fleet Manager, Captain John Ryder, telling me that another crew had had a problem with climbing out after two unsuccessful approaches into Leeds. They had had to use their combined strength to persuade the aircraft to climb and then had diverted to Manchester, which had better weather and a longer runway which enabled a shallower approach to be made. After exhaustive checks the Dan-Air engineers had found a small indent on the tail plane surfaces, indicating that a stone had probably been picked up whilst the aircraft was taxiing past some work in progress. It is mandatory to check the flying controls for full and free movement before take-off. It was thought that the stone had started embedding itself during the moving of the elevators, preventing the final completion of the full movement. The impairment was not noticed during a gentle climb and smooth flight, but had become apparent during the two unsuccessful approaches into Leeds.

It was only on the first overshoot when a marked change of pull up attitude was necessary that the stone really began jamming the elevators. Thinking it could be ice, which would melt, a second approach was made but the weather had not improved and the second overshoot embedded the stone even more, so brute force was needed by both pilots to make the aircraft climb. The diversion to Manchester was flown very carefully. I was assured that the aircraft had been very thoroughly tested after the stone had disappeared, and was asked to fly it back to Luton. I then realised why the removal of stones from the taxiways and runways at Stornoway was important not only for aircraft tyres! Thereafter we made quite sure that we very carefully checked that we had completely full and free movement of the controls before every take-off.

....

I was posted back to Gatwick at the beginning of April 1973, having spent almost exactly a year based at Luton. It was so good to be 'home' again and be spared that journey to Luton and back. I had begun to wonder how much longer I could cope with it. To stave off tiredness when returning to Horsham by night I would turn up the volume of my little portable radio and, weather permitting, would open my window during the part of my drive down the soporific M1 motorway. At that time there was no M25 motorway circling London so I would lower the volume after turning off to drive through towns, built-up areas and when taking the short cut across Heathrow Airport past the hangars. Even though I turned it up again in the more open countryside, I would sometimes have to stop in a lay-by and stamp around the car to remain alert. Despite all this I twice found myself on the wrong side of the little lane near home! It was great just to have a twenty minute drive to Gatwick again and of course see more of my family.

My first flight from Gatwick was to Berne, the capital of Switzerland. As the airport has only a short runway and lies in a valley surrounded by mountains, I had flown there with a check captain earlier in the year to be shown the landing and take-off procedures. Our thrice weekly service into Berne was the only flight available from the UK so it was fortunate that on this occasion the weather was fine and the views stupendous.

On the 3rd April I flew the inaugural service to Tours in France. Tours has a really good long runway, but could also have weather problems. Some days one flew to both Tours and Berne, on other days these two destinations were interspersed with flights to

Ashford and Beauvais for Paris, as Dan-Air had taken over Skyways in 1971.

Skyways was initially based at Lympne but was then relocated to Lydd near Ashford. As well as the one to Beauvais, they operated several other services and their 748 aircraft enabled the Link City Service to be extended from Bournemouth to Leeds and Glasgow. Their schedules to Jersey and Guernsey continued from Bournemouth in addition to those from Lydd and Swansea. Another connection with Amsterdam was introduced with a regular service from Teeside in the north. We flew some of these in turn.

Some of the Skyways pilots joined Dan-Air, among them two women First Officers, Gillian Cazelet and Delphine Gray-Fiske. I understand that Gillian's father had not been keen on her becoming a pilot so she had worked at a petrol filling station in order to pay for her licences. She had become a survey pilot before joining Skyways. I think Delphine had been luckier; becoming a flying instructor had been her stepping stone to airline flying.

As Dan-Air was the first airline to have three women pilots, it was decided we would make our uniform a little less masculine by changing the tie for a neat cravat We already had the Women's Royal Air Force style jacket and hat, but trousers, rather than a skirt were deemed to be the most practical. In the meanwhile Marilyn Booth had been accepted into the new Dan-Air Sponsorship Scheme to train for her Commercial Pilot's Licence. She had obtained her Private Pilot's Licence whilst in Australia and had started with the Company as an air hostess. After showing her keenness, she had been recommended for sponsorship by the Captains with whom she had flown. She was the first woman to be accepted into the Scheme and passed through with flying colours. And so we became four! Marilyn and I, indeed, made history as the first all female crew in Britain when we flew together from Gatwick to Bristol, then Beauvais and back to Gatwick on the 12th April 1974, but it was kept quiet at the time. Thank goodness. We had had enough publicity!

....

Shortly afterwards, like a bolt from the blue, a completely unexpected letter arrived advising me that I had been chosen to receive the Whitney Straight Award. The ceremony would be conducted at the Royal Aeronautical Society and the Award presented by Her Royal Highness Princess Anne on the 20th May 1974. I learnt that the Award had been donated by Mr Whitney Straight in 1967 to 'recognise the achievements and status of women in aviation, either by a single achievement of exceptional merit or, by a history of consistent and valuable contributions by British women active in any aspect of aviation, flying, scientific research, factory or administration work or in the Armed Forces'. The Award consisted of a sculpture cast in bronze by Dame Barbara Hepworth, and £200. I was stunned and became more and more nervous as the weeks went by. To add to my nervousness, the Company heard of it and Miguel and I were invited to the Dan-Air Annual Dinner in London, and found ourselves at the top table. Both the Chairman and Mrs Newman were very interested in finding out what flying the scheduled services was like and were perhaps surprised to learn that in order to save time on the several turnarounds the Captain could be in the cockpit for nearly nine hours during a day's flying. The co-pilot would do the external checks whilst the Captain completed the paperwork and internal checks. While I was talking to Mr Newman, Miguel asked the orchestra to play a Spanish quickstep and invited Mrs Newman to dance! Intrepid as ever, he probably taught her how to name the fingers on her hand in Spanish during the evening. He was happily remembered for doing this on other occasions.

Returning to the ceremony at the Royal Aeronautical Society, I had no idea how big it would be. Having been asked to send a list of guests I would like to invite, I only requested tickets for my near family and for people who had helped me. Among these were Charles Argles who had been instrumental in my joining Mortons, Freddie Laker who had saved me, Bob Atkins who had accepted me into Dan-Air and Jock Hunter who had been my mentor all along the way.

I later found that over a hundred and forty people were invited. Among the official guests were the Chairmen of the Civil Aviation Authority and British Airports Authority, the President and Vice President of the Royal Aeronautical society, many past Presidents and officials and the Presidents of other aviation associations, as well as members of the Selection Panel who had chosen me, one of them being John Cunningham, Chief Comet Test Pilot and wartime ace, whom I had admired throughout the War, never dreaming that I would fly his wonderful Comet. Air Commodore Allott (WRAF) and Group Captain and Mrs Douglas Bader were also invited.

Charles and Margaret Argles kindly drove me up to London for the ceremony. I spent the whole of the journey practising my acceptance speech in my mind. All I could say was how honoured I was to be chosen and grateful for the opportunity given me to follow in the tradition of the early pioneers and marvellous women who had flown during the War. There had been times when things were difficult, but no one appreciated anything without a challenge. I also wanted to thank all the people, among them many men, who had helped and guided me along the way.

I was wound up so tightly that the ceremony passed in a blur. The citation said "For exceptional courage and determination, under difficult circumstances, in the pursuit of a career with the highest qualifications in aviation". All I can remember is that the Princess looked cool and composed in a beautifully simple cream dress trimmed with delicate embroidery. She afterwards admitted that she was not as keen on flying as her brother. Knowing that her favourite horse had just suffered an accident, I tried to express my real sympathy. I didn't have time to talk to many people, but I was very proud of how smart my sons and Miguel looked. As far as I was concerned, flying was something I just had to do. Mr Whitney Straight was warmly courteous and understanding.

Very much later I learned just how honoured I was to have received the Whitney Straight Award. Whitney Straight had learnt to fly and had accumulated 60 hours flying time before he was sixteen, too young to have a licence. Whilst an undergraduate at Cambridge University he became interested in motor racing at which he excelled and won several championships, but his abiding passion remained aviation. In his early twenties he founded the Straight Corporation and developed airfields throughout Britain, starting several flying clubs, amongst them Exeter. He took over Western Airways, with its world record of 58 services a day, and designed and helped develop the Miles Whitney Straight two-seater aeroplane. By 1938 he operated 40 aircraft and employed over 160 people. After joining the County of London Squadron of the Auxiliary Air Force early in 1939, he was called up into Fighter Command at the outbreak of war. However, due to his experience in establishing airfields, he was sent to Norway in 1940 to find suitable landing sites for our aircraft. He mobilised the local populace into clearing snow from frozen lakes, but unfortunately the Germans bombed the day after some of our Gladiator aircraft had landed. Seriously injured and temporarily deafened, he was evacuated by the Navy. For this work he was later awarded the Military Cross.

Whilst recovering he became Personal Assistant to the Duke of Kent but as soon as he was fit he rejoined his Squadron and fought with them during the Battle of Britain. He became a Flight Commander early in 1941 and in the April was posted to command another squadron. He was awarded the Distinguished Flying Cross for having destroyed and damaged several aircraft and for having shown excellent qualities of leadership and zeal.

His luck ran out during an attack on a destroyer at Fécamp on the last day of July 1941. He was shot down by flak and made a forced landing in a field. He had always been prepared by wearing a civilian jacket over his uniform and civilian boots, as well as carrying money and a pistol. He bought a hat from a farmer, slept in hay in a barn occupied by German soldiers and made his way to Paris by train. While waiting for a connection at Rennes he wandered around the town where he found a house requisitioned for the Germans and dropped an English penny through the letter box! On reaching Paris he found the American Embassy closed, but traced the caretaker who gave him some money. With this he made his way to the border between Occupied and Vichy France. He swam a river to cross over but unfortunately was eventually imprisoned posing as a British Army Officer. He managed to escape in June 1942 and, with the help of the Resistance, reached a beach near Perpignan, from where he was rowed out to a trawler which took him and other fugitives to Gibraltar. He reached England on July 21st 1942. It had taken him almost exactly a year.

By this time it was realised that air transport was increasingly vital in the Middle East and he was sent to command 216 Squadron at the newly developed Cairo Airport. His organisation was so efficient that it was adopted as the pattern for Transport Command. In 1945 he took command of 45 Group in Europe, which was attached to the British Air Force of Occupation and finally left the service as an Air Commodore. He became Deputy Chairman of British European Airways, Managing Director,

Deputy Chairman, Executive Vice Chairman and finally Chairman of the British Overseas Airways Corporation. He also became Executive Chairman of Rolls Royce and was involved with many professional and business organisations such as the Air Registration Board, the Institute of Navigation, the Post Office Corporation, Midland Bank, Royal Aero Club, British Light Aircraft Centre, Royal Air Force Association and British Airline Pilots Association. And it was this man's Award that had been give to me! The honour was more incredible than I had realised. He also invited me to his home for tea and, when leaving, gave me a dozen freshly laid eggs for my family!

All this after I had been given the Sir Alan Cobham Award on obtaining the Air Line Transport Pilots Licence. I could not believe I had received this from such a wonderful pioneer of flight, who had proved air transport was viable by flying all around Europe and Africa as well as taking his little seplane to Australia and back, landing on the Thames in front of the Houses of Parliament. He had also introduced flying to so many people through his 'flying circus' and had invented in flight refueling.

....

It was a relief to get back to flying and not to have to worry about a speech, other than to the passengers, although I did have a slight problem in composing one in French! We were flying the Mayor and Mayoress of Agen back from a visit to Southampton and it took me all the way across the Channel to think of how to say "We are now passing over Dinard, the weather en route and at Agen is good and we hope to be landing at ....". I could only think in Spanish! It also took me almost a quarter of an hour to think in French when we had to night-stop in Brest after flying a ship's crew there.

Marilyn and I enjoyed several flights together, including one when we flew the Mayor and Mayoress of Brighton to Berne. We were also fêted by the Authorities, given a hug by the symbolic Bernese Bear and presented with a large box of chocolates and big bouquet of flowers. Although we had to turn round and fly back to Gatwick on that occasion, on another one I did have the opportunity of seeing the beautiful city of Berne, with its surprisingly wide streets and elegant buildings decorated with flowered balconies. It was after a night-stop due to a technical problem and I also remember with pleasure the invitation to a very good evening concert.

Landing at the airport of Berne could, however, be tricky in bad weather due to the surrounding mountains. Sometimes, even when snowing, strong winds caused one to have to use almost full power to counteract the gusts. If the weather was too bad we would have to divert to Basle. We didn't like doing it as we felt cheated and felt for the passengers having to do an extended journey. Even on good days the direction of the wind and the length of the short runway could decide the number of extra standby passengers one could take. If the wind was oscillating in different directions it could make things difficult, especially if one had a Ministry of Aviation Inspector on board checking everything! It happened to me when I was accompanied by one who had been a Captain I had flown with as a stewardess in Scottish Airlines! On the lighter side, I was surprised and amused when I was told I was number two to land after a very colourful airship one sunny afternoon. Even though it was a small one, it took precedence. As in Navel lore, 'steam gives way to sail'. We also had to watch out for it on take-off!

Charters to different destinations extended our 748 routes from Gatwick during 1974. We added Nantes, Reims, Rotterdam, Amsterdam, Kassel, Dusseldorf, Frankfurt and Hanover.

Weather could, of course, affect both charter and scheduled flights. If possible we always avoided thunderstorms and cumulonimbus clouds. Having reached the holding point for take-off from Ostend back to Gatwick to complete our scheduled flight, I saw on the cockpit radar that a long orange line of them had built up right across our departure path. I advised the poor passengers that it wasn't our evening for hurrying and that we would wait patiently until they had moved. I had seen that it extended too far north and south for a reasonable diversion. I think we had to wait for over a quarter of an hour before we could safely edge round to the north. Although we were all a little late for supper, the flight back was at least relatively smooth!

Ordinary cumulus could also give an uncomfortable ride. The flight from Lydd to Beauvais was a fairly short one and could be flown at a low level. Having been an air traffic controller I knew that the air-space below airways could be busy with unknown traffic and preferred to climb higher into the airway and be separated from known aircraft. However, returning from Beauvais one afternoon we encountered some bumpiness although the sky below us was clear of cloud and there was a lovely view of the pleasant green countryside towards the coast in the warm sunshine. I couldn't believe it when I looked up and saw high cumulus had appeared above us, much higher than usual, not making shadows on the ground. I could only ask to descend out of the airway to find a smoother level.

My last flight on the 748 was on the 25th February 1975 on the same route. After landing at Lydd I was asked to phone Gatwick. To my amazement I was told that I was posted onto the BAC 1-11 forthwith! I did my first supernumery flight on the aircraft to Munich three days later.

I had secretly hoped to return to my beloved Comet and had, in between my 748 flights, and on my days off, managed to fit in several on-going familiarization ones on the Comet. However, the Comet was always going to be made redundant as the larger 1-11 could carry the same number of passengers, 119, on only two engines instead of four. As it happened the tourist business built up so much that the fuel thirsty Comet was indeed kept in service for quite a few more years.

Chapter 19

BAC 1-11 Jet Captaincy

I was lucky this time as the BAC 1-11 course was held in the new Dan-Air's building near Horsham station, just down the road from where we lived so I was able to get home every night. However, we had to travel up to Luton to use the Court Line Aviation simulator. Fortunately it was a very good one – I was even able to land it, unlike some others!

From the history viewpoint, the One-Eleven was a short-range jet airliner of the 1960s and 1970s. Conceived by Hunting Aircraft, it was developed and produced by the British Aircraft Corporation when Hunting merged into BAC along with other British aircraft makers in 1960. The One-Eleven was designed to replace the Vickers Viscount on short-range routes.

Following the French Sud Aviation Caravelle, the BAC One-Eleven was the second short-haul jet airliner to enter service. This gave it the advantage of more efficient engines and previous jet-airliner experiences, making it a popular model; over half its sales at launch were to the largest and most lucrative market, the United States. The One-Eleven was one of the most successful British airliner designs and served until its widespread retirement in the 1990s due to noise restrictions. The 1-11 found itself in direct competition with the Douglas DC-9, and was joined by another competitor, the Boeing 737, only a year following its introduction. Advantages over the DC-9 included a cheaper unit cost. However the DC-9 offered more seating and its engines were interchangeable with those on the Boeing 727.

In Europe One-Elevens were common and was, in many respects, ideal for us to fly holidaymakers to Spain and as far afield as Greece. It continued in widespread use until the 1990s. Many One-Elevens then moved to smaller airlines, notably in the Far East and Africa.

During the course I managed more supernumery flights over weekends and, after passing the necessary exams, started six days of flying training, once again at Newcastle. On returning to Gatwick I put in more flights watching in the cockpit before being checked out on a flight to Rimini where I found that delicious ice creams were always brought out for the crew!

The only problem I had with the 1-11 was initially putting on too much bank in a turn, being used to the greater amount needed for a gentle turn on the slower 748. The line check captain was not best pleased! After several flights to various destinations with line captains, I finally flew on an observed flight with the Fleet Manager, Captain Spurrell, to Heraklion on the 16th of June. On approaching the airport I was too pre-occupied with positioning the aircraft downwind to take much notice of his announcement to the passengers. He told them that they were making history by flying with the first woman jet captain in the United Kingdom! When I heard them clapping after landing, I thought it was only because they had landed safely!

He didn't tell me what he had said until they had disembarked – and then he just added "I wouldn't let you loose unless I thought you were safe enough to fly my girlfriend around!"

I did my first actual 'solo' flight in command over the night of the 20th/21st June to Athens and back. At least with night flights there wasn't so much traffic and, thank goodness, the weather was reasonable. What a way to start! However, it was wonderful to be able to fly up around 30,000 feet again. It was so much clearer and more free – a long way above the earth's problems. Even the thunderstorms didn't normally ascend that high!

During the next five years I flew to many European capitals and cities, Mediterranean islands, North Africa and the Canary Islands. Among the many new destinations were Madrid, Lisbon, Geneva, Zurich, Nice, Naples, Palermo and Copenhagen, Oslo, Stockholm, Kristiansand and Bergen in Scandinavia, as well as Malta and Gibraltar. Needless to say I asked to fly to Menorca as often as possible – but other people wanted to go there too!

One of the favourite tourist destinations was Palma in

Majorca, and it was just before an evening flight from Gatwick that a passenger came on board all by himself. The chief hostess came up to the cockpit saying that she didn't know what was wrong with him – he was shaking from head to foot. I had only read about this in novels so didn't really believe it until when I went into the cabin. He really was shaking so much that he couldn't get a light anywhere near his cigarette! I asked if he had flown before and he managed to stutter that he had, and when I asked if the flight had been bumpy he nodded and said "ye-ess".

Having assured him that I had checked the weather and that it was going to be a smooth flight this time, I sat down beside him and just said that I had been flying for many years and was very much happier in the air than I was on the roads. He slowly started calming down, but I asked him if he was really that unhappy, was it worth putting himself through it? At that moment the other passengers started coming aboard so I quickly offered that, if he decided to remain with us, he would be very welcome to come up to the cockpit once we were airborne. He did so and then he asked the most intelligent questions of any passenger I had met, questioning me about the instruments and the procedures. When I asked what he did for a living, he turned out to be a long distance lorry driver! Fortunately it was a good flight, but over the Alps we had an air conditioning failure on one side. We had to descend as gently as possible so that he wouldn't notice!

Sadly the weather wasn't always calm in the Mediterranean. On one occasion there had been severe thunderstorms around Palma. Aircraft had had to divert to Barcelona because of the depth of water on the runway and the parking area being flooded. By the time we arrived conditions had improved over Majorca, but adjacent little Menorca was still being pounded and the north coast of Africa looked as though World War II was still on with continuous lightning flashes.

On the other hand, we could be lucky with the weather and would be able to see the countryside and beautiful scenery very clearly. Flying down the eastern coast of Italy, we could sometimes see for miles inland. The only problem was that passengers would ask for the names of every little town. We only knew the names of the nearest radio beacon. Sometimes they would coincide!

However, the most beautiful sight for me – and one I will never forget – was Concorde climbing effortlessly away to the east of us. She had followed us over Europe and whilst over land had been restricted and unable to climb to her levels. At last she was free! When the women pilots of the Ninety Nines had organized a visit to Filton to see over this wonderful aircraft, I had been unable to join them as I was flying myself. How I would have love to have flown her! I felt incredibly sad when she was taken out of service.

The view of the snow-capped mountains, the Alps or the Dolomites, could also be beautiful and awe-inspiring. I always used to enjoy pointing out Mont Blanc to the passengers when we flew from Berlin to Spain. However, I would occasionally wonder if we could land in a valley if necessary!

Similar to the Comet, the 1-11 flew holiday charters for the Berliners to the most popular tourist destinations and the crews would, in turn, spend three to five days based in Berlin. The hotel we used was not far from the station and bus park in front. Having been to Grunewald and Wansee while on the Comet, I would offer to take my crew for a river trip when we had any free time and the weather was kind. I preferred the bus as one could see more. It only took twenty minutes through the residential area with its wide streets lined with trees screening moderately tall blocks of flats and a few private houses.

On reaching Wansee we were able to walk a short way through the woods onto the steamer which cruised up and down the river. By this time the Wall had been completed on the eastern side.

We would cruise as far as a bridge crossing into Eastern Germany and up again on the western side. Although pleasant and relaxing on deck or in the lower covered seating area with its small bar, it was still eerie and forbidding to watch the sleek and menacing grey patrol boats moving up and down on the other side of the demarcation line in the middle of the river. The contrast had become even greater. On the western side there were more barges and pleasure steamers and the small sandy beaches were always filled with families enjoying themselves. To my amazement, wind surfers added their bright sail colours to the holiday atmosphere.

Most flights were long ones, but one Easter Sunday we had a very short, early one to an island off the south coast of Denmark. The weather was really good so on our return we took the steamer from Wansee to a well known park. It was a pleasure to see the Berliners just strolling among the spring flowers and the children enjoying playing in the warm sunshine. It snowed the next day but fortunately, I didn't have to fly!

My least favourite of the long flights was one to North Africa. On the way back we would have to fly more slowly for fuel economy. Before entering our Berlin corridor we had to have more fuel than usual so that we could divert down another corridor if need be. This increased our flight time and the fuel had to be checked very carefully en route. No one wanted to make an interim landing to pick up more fuel.

The flight to Berlin from Malaga was also a long one, especially against strong headwinds. Once the westerly winds were stronger than forecast and this was compounded by Air Traffic Control directing us to change to a lower level midway over Spain, causing us to use even more fuel. Fortunately, the visibility around Malaga was very good and we could see the airport and another aircraft well ahead of us from several miles to the north. On contacting the tower, I told them that we had the other aircraft in sight and would like to make a visual approach. I had heard that their Air Traffic Control had become very pedantic and was not at all impressed when we were told to go to their beacon and hold. I had enough fuel to do so, but wasn't going to waste it. To jerk the controller out of his rigid routine I replied that if we had to hold we would have to divert to Seville. This caused a blind panic and we were given an immediate direct clearance. Unfortunately, the other aircraft, already on its final approach, was told to overshoot. I was angry about it but not as angry as the other Captain. After we had both landed, I went over to the other Captain to say how sorry I was that he had had to overshoot and explain, but he would not accept my apology. Woman pilot! A few days later, I had to fly to Palma and was asked by the Station Manager as to why I landed at Malaga with a matchbox full of fuel? You can't win!

Malaga became associated with a few problems. On another

occasion, a completely different incident occurred. Just after take-off from Malaga on another fine day, a red light came on, indicating that a door wasn't correctly fastened. This time we had to go to the beacon to hold until we had used up enough fuel to be able to land without putting too much strain on the undercarriage and tyres. Once on the ground we found that the hatch cover to a compartment under the cockpit had worked loose. It had been put in the wrong way round at Gatwick. After our return, I suggested that an arrow be painted on the cover to indicate the correct direction, as on the 748. A baulk was instead then added to the cover so that it couldn't fit in the wrong way!

Malaga airport could also be affected by severe weather. On a day when I was due to fly there, planes had been diverting all morning due to bad thunderstorms which had remained in the area for some time. We were lucky and managed to land in a brief respite, but when our delayed passengers came on board, they argued about their seats. Once again I had to say: "This is your Captain speaking. Unless you sit down immediately, I cannot taxi this aircraft and we will lose our take-off slot. As the weather is deteriorating rapidly, you will have to spend the night in Malaga." They sat down. After take-off, the thunderstorms closed in again and formed a solid wall along the coast, extending inland to the west. I requested permission to stay out to sea and was just asked to report when I could turn inland towards our normal route. Our radar depicted an almost continuous area of severe turbulence and, despite a few requests, we were unable to do so. When we eventually came abeam Ibiza, a frustrated but understanding area controller suggested that we might like to change to the Balearic route which would take us to the east of Paris. We gratefully accepted and moved across to take the clearer route home.

Malaga did however come in useful at the time of a French Air Traffic Control strike. I was rostered to fly from Manchester to Menorca. As we were unable to fly direct over France, Operations suggested that we fly down the west Atlantic coast and then turn inland over Spain to route via Malaga where we could top up our fuel. After landing at Malaga, I decided to take on as much fuel as possible to cope with any problems. As we approached Palma, we were told 'Delay not determined' at Menorca, which meant that they could not tell us how long we would have to wait for landing clearance.

Menorca's parking area was small and completely full of aircraft. Until one was given take-off clearance, another could not land. The airways avoiding France were overloaded and the route clearance needed before take-off were greatly delayed. Palma asked if we would like to land and wait there, but as we had plenty of fuel, I decided to continue on to Menorca. In the early hours of the morning, we held over their beacon for nearly half an hour. I asked to remain as high as possible to conserve fuel and also make less noise. The holding pattern took us over Alcaufar and my dear Step-mother was on holiday down below with friends! After landing, I found that the harassed ground staff were at the end of their tether. I called the unhappy passengers together to sympathize with them and tried to tell them that the French Air Traffic Controllers' strike was for air safety. I explained the problem of having to re-route and promised we would get airborne as soon as possible. Fortunately the strike was over by the time my Step-mother had to fly back!

Any problems with Air Traffic Control caused many repercussions. British Air Traffic Control was considered by us to be the best in Europe – calm, competent and reassuring. However, when the assistants went on strike, the controllers had to cope with the work as well as their own, causing increased pressure and also consequent delays. Before flying to Menorca once again, I was told that French Air Traffic was trying to hold aircraft abeam Paris on the return journey and that I should instead continue on to Abbeville on the north coast as normal and from there contact British Air Traffic Control. On entering the hold at Abbeville, I asked the British controller for the latest delay information.

To my surprise he curtly asked why we should come on ahead of the aircraft holding below us. I immediately requested the call sign of the other aircraft and asked the other Captain how long he could hold. I was flying the smaller 1-11 with a full load of passengers, which meant that I had been unable to uplift extra fuel for a long hold and if this was necessary, would have to divert to Beauvais. He fortunately had more fuel and courteously allowed us to go on ahead. He was able to follow us shortly afterwards and when I went to his airline office to thank him, again I found that he was one of the Morton's skippers with whom I had flown!

Sometime later I was returning from Menorca as a passenger with Miguel, Jon and Chris after a pleasant holiday. After boarding the Comet, I went up to the cockpit to greet the Captain, who I knew. Another gentleman was there and was introduced as a colleague. He turned out to be the Air Traffic Controller who had been so brusque whilst I was in the holding pattern at Abbeville during the British Air Traffic Assistants strike. He humbly apologised, explaining the pressure of the extra work. I understood. This time, due to route congestion, our take off clearance was delayed and we had to wait on the aircraft for nearly an hour with the emergency windows open for ventilation. He learnt about the other side of the coin.

Chapter 20

Bomb Scares And Other Excitements

Other things that can happen .....

Many airlines had bomb scares but they were never mentioned. Just before Christmas 1977, one of our aircraft landed at Frankfurt with a supposed bomb on board. The increased security meant that we and the following Dan-Air aircraft were parked away from other airlines. I was rostered to fly there on Boxing night, the 26th December, to pick up some passengers for England. It turned out to be one of those nights. During her check of the cabin before leaving Gatwick, the chief hostess discovered that only half the passenger oxygen masks were the correct size for our aircraft. If there should be a pressurization failure at cruising level, half the passengers would be starved of oxygen. Correct replacements were not available, but as there were no passengers on the outbound flight and there was sufficient oxygen for the crew, Operations suggested we fly to Frankfurt at our normal height but returned with the passengers at 10,000 feet. This was the normal maximum for breathing without oxygen but meant using a great deal more fuel.

After landing at Frankfurt, we were directed to a far off solitary stand behind a long terminal finger next to a Police office. While waiting for our passengers, I noticed police vans cutting across the corner of our designated area. Once the passengers were safely aboard, I requested push back clearance. Instead of a slight forward and aft jerk, which could be felt when a tug started to push, there was a definite sideways jerk. I stopped everything and went down to find that a van had driven into our starboard wing tip! The driver said that the ice warning light had dazzled him!

This light shines along the leading edge of the wing to show up any icing and is supposed to delineate it on the ground. The collision had caused a dent in the wing tip, but fortunately clear of the navigation light and above the driver's head. However, it had destroyed one of our lightning conductors. I had to walk through the passenger terminal finger, across the terminal building and halfway into the opposite finger to phone our Operations and engineers at Gatwick from the agent's office. I had somehow strained my back a couple of days before so had hoped for an uneventful and peaceful flight! Fortunately, the engineers confirmed that it would be safe for us to fly back, but suggested that we avoid thunderstorms. This we did, flying well to the north and at 10,000 feet all the way, using an incredible amount of fuel. I was glad to get home that night!

The only other time I had to fly the 1-11 back at 10,000 feet was after a windscreen heater failed on my side whilst flying over the Alps above 30,000 feet en-route to Sardinia with families going home for Christmas. As the very low outside air temperature could have caused the windscreen to crack and a real problem, I decided to divert to Milan in Italy. No-one was expecting us in the early hours but, after being called out, the restaurant manager at the airport provided our poor tired and bemused passengers with Italian Christmas cake – the only food available. I was very grateful.

Having phoned Gatwick to advise them of our predicament, we had to wait for a relief aircraft, crew and engineers. Only one of the hostesses complained – she wasn't really suitable for the job and didn't last long. The passengers were flown on to their destination and I only hoped that they would manage to enjoy their Christmas. As the engineers were unable to repair our windscreen, we flew back at low level, avoiding the Alps, and the First Officer enjoyed some map reading! The French countryside did look beautiful in the clear morning sunlight.

I was also greatly impressed by another gentleman, but this time it was in Venice. We were half-way down our final approach when Air Traffic Control told us that the ground handling staff had just gone on strike, and that we could expect an unknown delay. After landing I suggested to the passengers that the able-bodied male passengers could help myself and the First Officer unload the baggage from the holds under the aircraft and that we would then assist in taking the suitcases to the terminal building, and that the hostesses would help the other passengers there. We had just started unloading when, out of the corner of my eye, I saw a baggage trolley snaking across towards us, steered by a very slight man. He said he had come to help us. We gratefully accepted his assistance, and after the passengers and their luggage were safely in the terminal, I stopped him as he was coming back from another aircraft to thank him again and give him a gratuity. He would not accept it, saying "No, no .. I am the Airport Manager."! We had to wait another hour for the strike to end so that the toilets could be emptied, but I will never forget him.

On a completely different occasion, when climbing out from Venice towards the Alps and home, we were asked by Swiss Air Traffic Control if we could see any unusual lights in the sky. Passing through broken cloud at 15,000 feet we suddenly saw several coloured lights grouped together a little higher up to the west. Red and green could be from aircraft signalling pistols, but there were other colours as well and fireworks could not possibly reach that height. Something unknown had been noticed on radar and aircraft in the area were being asked to report. Was it a U.F.O., an Unidentified Flying Object? It remained a mystery. Sometime earlier, Portuguese Air Traffic had asked aircrew flying near Lisbon if they could see anything unusual just out to sea moving slowly north along the coast. Several crews and passengers saw brown cigar shaped objects quite clearly at about their own levels. It was later promulgated that they were scientific meteorology balloons!

During 1978, I had to have a hysterectomy operation which put me out of use for a while. Whilst in hospital, some amusing cards arrived from fellow pilots, one congratulating me on being the first 1-11 Captain to be 'speyed'. The 1-11 had Rolls Royce Spey engines! My gynaecological specialist had been brought up on an R.A.F. airfield and had wanted to fly. He seemed more interested in the fact that I was a pilot than that I needed surgery! In fact, he asked if I could give him a flight in a cockpit which, at a later date, I was able to do. During the flight we were delayed en route to Menorca, so he also learnt something about airline flying!

Rolls-Royce engines are famous for being amongst the best in the world, but the Spey engine could very occasionally develop a small problem on starting. There was a certain small part near the casing and cowling which could stick in the wrong position and would be freed by a firm tap on the adjacent engine casing. This also happened on the Magister, the light aircraft on which I had learned to fly. In those days, one carried a rounded stone in one's flying suit as a hammer! Inconveniently, the problem occurred again at Barcelona, when we had to take over the aircraft which had come from Berlin and fly it to Las Palmas in the Canary Islands. The crew reported that they had had a little difficulty in starting one of the engines. After the passengers had boarded, we hopefully tried to start the affected port engine, but it would not oblige. The First Officer and I had to descend the front stairs and lift up the cowling. No other problems were visible so I sent him back for the crash axe from the cockpit, which he duly applied to the appropriate spot. It worked! What the passengers thought I do not know! I wasn't going to risk it again, so at Las Palmas we started the engine before the passengers boarded. We weren't supposed to do so, but I didn't want another pantomime and more dismayed clients. Needless to say, it started very happily without a problem! To make up for the engine behaving itself, the autopilot went on strike, so we had to take turns in hand flying the aircraft all the way back to Barcelona. Because I couldn't keep the passengers strapped in for the three and a quarter hour flight, we had to constantly keep adjusting for any movement. Fortunately, the hostesses were slight, so their movement up and down the cabin reduced the 'porpoising' effect. It seemed a long flight!

....

One never knows what will happen next. A complete change of hemisphere and climate occurred early in 1979. Out of the grey skies of February came an invitation to be guest speaker at the Annual Convention of the Australian Women Pilots Association to be held in Perth, Western Australia, early in March to celebrate the 100th Anniversary of the founding of the city. I was surprised and honoured and was granted some leave and hastily found some summer clothing. Sadly, Miguel was unable to come, but he and Chris saw me off at Heathrow on an arranged courtesy British Airways flight. It was a long overnight flight broken only by refuelling stops. To my surprise, the Chief Steward was one I had worked with as a stewardess! As usual I was unable to sleep, so spent a lot of time in the cockpit and was invited to be there for the approach and landing into Sydney at 6am local time. I will always remember the view and was amazed at the number of interweaving waterways around the city. 'Venice of the South'!

The flight had been arranged through the travel departments of British Airways and Dan-Air, but between them they had forgotten that I needed a visa! After landing, I was hauled into the Immigration Office and treated like a naughty school girl. I was only allowed to stay in the country as I, fortunately, had the invitation letter in my handbag. I was, however, only given ten days! It had never crossed my mind that I would need a visa for Australia. Australia is part of the British Commonwealth! If it had been South Africa, which had become a Republic, I might have thought about it!

Although the Convention was to be held in Perth, I had asked to fly to Sydney first to see my youngest sister, Marcelle, who, with her husband and son, had emigrated to Australia. They were waiting for me and wondering what on earth had happened. It was great to see them again and all I could do was apologise! After recovering from jet lag, I was taken sightseeing. I sat on the steps of the famous Opera House, but alas, wasn't allowed in. We took a boat trip under the amazing Sydney Harbour Bridge and walked in the quiet green central park. At that time, the skyscrapers weren't too high and I liked the city very much. But, surprisingly, was disappointed by Bondi Beach. It was smaller than I had imagined the sand not as white nor the rollers as big.

I was very sad to leave my family but had to reach Perth when expected and was able to persuade Ansett, the internal airline, to give me a discount on their flight via Melbourne. In my ignorance, I had not realised how big and wide Australia is and would not have believed that it would take about four hours. I had imagined it to be more like South Africa, but the internal desert area was very, very much bigger! I then understood why British Airways had, at first, seemed reluctant to alter my ticket to Sydney!

I managed to talk my way into the cockpit and the pilots were quite pleasant. They did not have any women airline pilots at that time, which was surprising as Australia had some famous women pilots. Robyn Miller was one, who as a nurse with the Flying Doctor Service, was fondly known as 'The Sugarbird Lady' as she flew around the outback dispensing anti-polio vaccine on sugar lumps! Another very experienced pilot was Beryl Young who was the pilot for the Premier of Queensland.

I was given a warm welcome on arrival and driven to a big hotel on the outskirts of the city where most of the people attending the Convention were staying. The first day was taken up with a tree-lined river trip, during which we stopped to look round some historic houses. The trees reminded me of South Africa and the houses of southern America. The next day, coaches took us to an Air Force base, where we were able to look over and sit in some of the aircraft which I would love to have flown. A cross-country flying competition was also organized from a civil airfield, where a parked Dakota and Tiger Moth brought back many memories. Fortunately, I was only asked to be an observer in a four seater, so was able to relax a little and enjoy the scenery. I don't think we won, but I was greatly impressed by the high standard of flying by the Australian women.

On the business day of the Convention, I was invited to have lunch at an open air restaurant. The friendly conversation overran time and I became a little concerned that we would be late for the meeting. I hate being late for anything, airline flying making one very conscious of good time keeping! As a guest, I felt awkward and we had to slip in quietly after it had started. I was feeling guilty so made a near fatal mistake at the beginning of my speech saying how pleased and honoured I was to be with them for the celebration of the 100th Anniversary of the founding of 'Sydney' – hastily correcting it to 'Perth' – making the excuse that I had just been with my sister! I had no idea that there was great rivalry between the two cities and it was only because I was a 'Pommie' that I was forgiven! All I could do then was tell them my own history, that Dan-Air had four women pilots and that British Airways had started recruiting women. Indeed B.A. subsequently poached Dan-Air's already trained women!

Little did I know it but my talk was being recorded and I was later asked for permission for it to be used for members unable to attend the Convention at Perth and perhaps for a meeting of the Equal Opportunities Board. I had heard that one of the members, Deborah Wardley, had applied to Ansett with all the necessary qualifications, but that she had been rejected on the grounds that she would marry and could have children. This was always the major stumbling block for women. Not all women marry and have children. Some widows need to support their children and a nanny/housekeeper. Any time taken off during pregnancy could be the same as that required by a male pilot for illness and convalescence.

The re-training needed could be similar and less expensive than training a new pilot – provided sufficient experience had been gained. Nowadays, married pilots in British Airways are able to arrange their rosters to take it in turn to be with their children and help the nanny/housekeeper – but it took a long time! Deborah Wardley was finally accepted and Marilyn Booth, who had been trained by Dan-Air and had formed the all women crew with me, later flew also with Ansett, when she returned to Australia.

At the end of the Convention, I greatly appreciated the invitation of my kind hostess, Helen Henderson and her husband, John, to stay on for a couple of days in their pleasant home on the seashore and was able to enjoy a swim in the refreshing breakers – much nicer than Bondi! This was followed by flying down to an airshow. A number of light aircraft were involved and my pilot was keen to do some aerobatics en route. He started with a slow roll: I hadn't been upside down for a long while and wasn't sure if I would have preferred a flick roll! I enjoyed the airshow on the small coastal airfield until I was asked if I would like to join him in cutting the toilet roll competition. Never volunteer – I didn't, but couldn't say no! After throwing the roll out of the aircraft, the pilot aims to attack it in a series of steep descending turns trying to cut the trailing paper into as many pieces as possible. He had been a Luftwaffe pilot and it was seriously reminiscent of a dog fight!

Time had passed all too quickly and before I knew it I was checking in at Perth Airport for my return flight. Whilst doing so a young British First Officer came over and said "You taught me to fly the Dakota!" I hadn't actually done so, but had been the safety pilot when he had been checked out on a Morton's DC3. I was then invited to be in the cockpit for the night take-off, which was beautiful, some of the time en-route and, much later, for the early morning arrival at Heathrow. Incredibly the same Chief Steward was on duty for the second half of the flight. The aviation world is a small one!

None of my family were able to meet me so I returned home by coach and bus. The underground tunnel to the coach stop at Heathrow seemed endless, but I didn't have too long to wait. However, the route of the last bus meant that I had to walk a few blocks. It was rather a weary woman who trudged down the road with a suitcase in tow. At least it wasn't raining! There was no-one at home so I was able to sleep off some jet lag before Miguel and Chris returned from work. It was good to be back, but I will never forget the kindness and wonderful hospitality I had been given – except for the Sydney Immigration Officer – and how impressed I was by the Australian women pilots.

....

Just a month later, on the 16th of April whilst flying out of Berlin, we had a bomb scare. It was going to be one of those days. Before taking-off it was found, yet again, that the toilets on the aircraft were reluctant to flush. Our schedule for the day was to fly to the Balearic Islands, first to Palma in Majorca and then on to Ibiza before returning to Berlin in the afternoon. Having been advised that there had been a problem with the front passenger door, I asked my co-pilot to help with the opening after landing at Palma – I didn't want a stewardess hurting herself. The door opened without much difficulty, but I repeated the request at Ibiza, where it proved to be more awkward.

Our pleasant agent made it a quick turnaround, but at the last minute asked me to take an extra passenger and told me that his luggage would be put in the front hold under the cockpit. Shortly after our take-off for the return flight to Berlin a message on a piece of toilet paper was given to a loader at Ibiza. It was passed from person to person until it eventually reached someone in authority who finally contacted our Dan-Air agent. It stated that there was a bomb on our aircraft which would explode between 1500 – 1530 hours. She immediately phoned Dan-Air Operations at Gatwick. The call only reached them in time to try to contact us through Swiss Air Traffic Control, but we had just passed over the border into German airspace. It was the German controller who asked us to change frequency and passed on the basic message. I immediately thought a bomb could have been put in the front baggage hold under the cockpit! I learnt the details later. He suggested we might like to land at the nearest airport, Stuttgart. I whole heartedly agreed! I had recently checked the half hourly weather broadcast for German airfields and its report had been reasonable. As there was a time difference between Britain, Spain and Germany, we were unsure what time was meant, but it was 1500 hours our time! The upper controllers were very good giving us headings to steer out of the airway and down towards

Stuttgart. I told the passengers that we would be making a technical stop and asked the Chief Hostess to come up to the cockpit. I warned her of the problem, but told her not to inform the passengers initially. I didn't want a panic. We had a plane full of families with young children returning from their holidays.

On each change of controller, I asked that the Fire Service should be standing by the runway. During the descent I heard an aircraft reporting icing in cloud at 10,000 feet and realised that a front must have moved in very quickly. The weather had deteriorated rapidly. On contacting Stuttgart we were given a low cloud base with rain. They didn't seem too pleased at having to cope. When we were on a long base leg they suddenly told us to go away and hold over one of their beacons. I replied 'Negative – this is an emergency and we are coming straight in!' They reluctantly agreed and we continued our approach. Once more I asked for the Fire Service to be positioned near the runway – as it would have been at Gatwick.

I had only heard of trembler type bombs and thought I must do the smoothest landing possible on the wet runway, touching down as close to the beginning of the runway as possible. I couldn't risk jerking the aircraft with reverse thrust and could only rely on gentle braking before reaching the end.

Having previously landed at Stuttgart, I knew there was a military area on the south side and expected to be guided towards it, away from the normal civil parking area. Not only was there no Fire Service in sight, but we were instructed to turn towards the civil terminal and had to pass behind a long row of airliners and park between them and several light aircraft! After another request from me, we were finally followed by a fire vehicle. I was absolutely furious but had to think of my passengers and the aircraft.

While taxiing I sent the First Officer back to make sure the front door would open quickly and help with the evacuation of the passengers. Just before landing, the Hostess had briefed them on the bomb scare and had told them to leave the aircraft in an orderly way – which they fortunately did. As soon as possible, I went back to check that there was no-one left in the toilets. When I returned to the cockpit, I found the co-pilot doing the rundown checks. I just said "OUT!" I learnt afterwards that he had been castigated for leaving the switches on after a crash in the Air Force!

We went immediately to our agent's office from where I phoned Air Traffic to find out why they had wanted us to hold away from the airport. The reason given was that the bomb disposal team was engaged with another scare in the north of Germany and hadn't arrived yet! When they did, they found nothing on the aircraft. It was just another hoax!

In the meanwhile our poor passengers had been harshly treated by Customs. The Chief Hostess was almost in tears when she told me that they wouldn't allow even the women and children to go to the toilets. I went over at once and told the officers it was nothing to do with these passengers and to allow them to go into the terminal immediately. I was really angry! Thank goodness suicide female bombers were unheard of then!

Another problem had occurred en route. A generator had failed and this meant that we could not fly at night. If the other generator failed we would be in complete darkness. By the time the Bomb Squad had arrived and cleared the aircraft it was too late for us to continue our flight in daylight. Another crew and two engineers were flown to Stuttgart so that our poor passengers could finally reach their destination. Having run out of duty hours we also flew back as passengers. As we boarded the aircraft we were embarrassed to be applauded. Fortunately they didn't bear us a grudge.

On our return to England we attended a bomb course, during which we were told of plastic bombs which could be sealed in a match box and bombs which could be pre-set while climbing through a certain altitude to detonate on descent through that same altitude. I was glad I didn't know about them at the time! I later learnt that our threat had come from a mentally handicapped person who was disenchanted with airlines!

....

The only other generator failure I had occurred one afternoon half way across the English Channel en route to Sardinia. I told the passengers that we had to return to Gatwick to have it replaced as there were no spares at Sardinia and we could not fly our returning passengers back safely at night. While disembarking, an aggrieved gentleman complained bitterly. I quietly explained again and told him that we would also like to return home safely to our families at the end of the day. After the generator was repaired and the passengers returned on board he put his head round the cockpit door and just said "You've won"! I couldn't help wondering what names he might have been calling me in the meantime. Whilst attempting to improve conditions for aircraft and passenger safety as an Air Traffic Controller, I had overheard "It's that bloody woman again" and "I'm glad I'm not married to her!" More gallantly, in the air, I had been greeted with "Hello luv", which I enjoyed, or addressed as Mrs Ivan, Mrs Whyvone, Mrs Eevon and Mrs Poppay. Barcelona control started with "Ola guapa" (Hello pretty girl) until I jokingly said in Spanish, "My husband is Menorcean and very jealous!" After that it was "Ola Señora Sintes" which was very pleasant. At least we received good clearances! A few words in Spanish could be a help or a hindrance.

During another air traffic go-slow, several aircraft, including ours, were delayed at Palma. Although we had air conditioning from our auxiliary power unit, our passengers were becoming restive. I suggested that those who wished could walk around the aircraft, but remain close to it and be ready at a moment's notice to return inside if we received a surprise clearance. After continuing to wait patiently for a while, I politely asked in Spanish if the tower could tell me how much longer we might be delayed. I was given an immediate clearance, all in Spanish, to the dismay of my First Officer. Fortunately I knew the departure route off by heart. Our passengers on the tarmac had to hurry back to their seats!

As far as a hindrance was concerned, it occurred at Gatwick. Dan-Air started a weekly flight to Madrid for a Spanish agency. I foolishly imagined all the passengers would be Spanish and when one of the gauges under-read as I opened up the throttles for take-off, I explained in Spanish that we would have to return to the terminal for the problem to be corrected. The Chief Hostess rushed up to the cockpit to ask if I would explain in English to the English speaking passengers!

I enjoyed speaking some Spanish as Miguel was a patient teacher, even though he didn't find English all that easy. All our family holidays were spent in Menorca where the boys tried out their smattering of Spanish too. When my step-mother had to sell Casita Teresa, I wasn't able to buy it, but fortunately friends did so and the 'Sage' of the village advised us to buy a long piece of land near the top of Alcaufar. It had been used as a market garden and had a one-roomed cottage with a lean-to car port but, most importantly, had water rights to an adjacent well. He actually said, "Beg, borrow or steal!" We did the first two and slowly converted the car port into two rooms and then a tool shed into an indoor toilet and bathroom. Much later we made the cottage into a rambling farm house.

Menorca fortunately didn't suffer from many bush fires during the heat of the summer, but the mainland did. Pilots were asked to report on any seen from the air, especially those in isolated areas. Returning from the south one afternoon, we had noticed quite a few, and the following evening, flying south again, we saw a huge fire to our left. Just as we were about to report it, we realized that it was the reflection of the setting sun on Lake Geneva! Sunsets can be beautiful, but also deceptive.

Although the weather in the Mediterranean is often thought of as warm and calm throughout the year, it can be very unpredictable and suddenly change, especially in the autumn and winter. Although the prevailing wind over Menorca is from the north, when the wind came from the south and the visibility was good, I liked to position the aircraft along the northern coast so that the passengers could enjoy the enchanting scenery of the bays and creeks, many of them still completely unspoilt. However, bad weather with low cloud prevailed one afternoon and I had to make an instrument approach from the south to break cloud at the permitted height in time to see the runway and make a visual circuit at low level to land into the southerly wind. I hated having to thunder over the little villages and hoped they would forgive me!

During the winter quite a few flights were to Scandinavia as we had a service from Gatwick to Bergen in Norway, via Newcastle. It would be good to climb above the grey clouds into the clear blue skies and have sun all the way, but we would have to let down though the heavy dark clouds to almost ground level. Sometimes we were lucky and on clear days the views were stunningly beautiful. On the whole, these flights were without incident, except for one which had nothing to do with the weather. The aircraft we were flying had had a problem with the undercarriage and a special indicator box had been fitted in the cockpit. All went well until our return take-off from Bergen, when the box didn't indicate correctly. We triple checked everything we could and knew from the way the aircraft handled that the undercarriage was up. Fortunately we arrived back at Newcastle with enough daylight for us to do a fly past the control tower so that the controllers could check that the undercarriage was definitely down for landing. Before continuing, I phoned Operations at Gatwick, who suggested that I flew all the way back with the wheels down. Luckily I was flying the only type of 1-11 which was permitted to do so. We would have to fly more slowly in order not to damage the undercarriage and would again have to avoid thunderstorms. We flew the long way round, re-routing to the west.

Fortunately the weather was really good when I had to fly to Palma late in December and we had Freddie Laker as a passenger. His own airline didn't have a flight down there that day and he wanted to celebrate New Year in Majorca. I didn't know he was on board until he asked permission to come up to the cockpit and bounded in staying for quite a long while. I almost became concerned for his wife whom he had left alone in the cabin.

On arrival at Palma I was determined to do a really smooth landing and nearly used up two thirds of their long runway. I'm sure I didn't impress him at all!

Freddie Laker had started work in aviation as a mechanical engineer, becoming a Flight Engineer with Air Transport Auxiliary during World War II. After the end of the war, he worked for a short time with British European Airways and London Aero Motor Services, but in 1947 started his own business, Aviation Traders, as a war surplus dealer. He was based at Southend and specialised in converting bombers and transport aircraft into freighters. His business flourished when the Soviet blockade of West Berlin needed every possible aircraft to fly the 'Berlin Airlift' to take essential supplies to the Berliners.

In 1951 he took over his first airline, Air Charter, which was based at London's old Croydon Airport, but Aviation Traders at Southend continued to convert airframes and engines into various aircraft for operators around the world. It also produced a completely new aircraft design. In the same year its sister company won a contract to manufacture wing sections for Bristol freighters which was the aircraft Laker initially used to start his second airline, Channel Air Bridge, flying cars and their owners from Southend to Calais in 1954. This aircraft was superseded by another conversion – the Carvair which raised the cockpit above the fuselage, creating more space for cars.

By the end of 1958 he had decided to sell all three companies to Airwork, which then merged with Hunting Clan to form British United Airways, B.U.A., and he became their managing director from 1960 to 1965. British United was the first independent airline to completely equip with jet aircraft, the BAC 1-11 and the beautiful VC10 with which Laker was able to transfer the rights for the South American route from BOAC to B.U.A. and make a profit after BOAC had been making a loss. However, after a disagreement with the Chairman, Laker decided to leave and set up his own airline in 1966.

He used BAC 1-11s, Boeing 707s and a couple of Bristol Britannia's with which he started. He then became the first in Europe to buy the wide-bodied DC10s. Although he concentrated mainly on charter flying, he will always be remembered for 'Skytrain' which enabled ordinary people to fly across the Atlantic at a third of the price charged by established airlines. It was a daily scheduled DC10 flight from London to New York based on a 'first come – first served' seat with no frills. It was the first of its kind and was bitterly resented and contested, taking two years to gain bureaucratic approval which was finally given in 1977. It was a great success and led to further expansion and, in 1978, Freddie Laker was given a knighthood.

He was the first to order the wide-bodied European Airbus airliner. However the company had expanded too quickly, borrowing at too high an interest rate without enough financial backup to withstand a determined conspiracy to put it out of business by large airlines in Europe and America who were trying to copy Laker's discount fares. The airline was made bankrupt in 1982.

Undeterred, Freddie tried to re-launch the company with strong public support – including mine – but it wasn't until the 1990s that he was able to start another airline, his last, in the Bahamas, which lasted until 2005.

He was an incredible entrepreneur and a tough business man, but also was a caring person who helped anyone working with him if there was a problem.

When he heard that one of his pilots had cancer he wanted to send him to the best specialist he knew and kept in touch with him, even taking the time to send a telegram on the day Skytrain was launched saying that he knew the pilot would have wanted to be there but would see him soon. He had been invited but couldn't manage it. After he died, Freddie attended the funeral and offered all the services of the company and a flight on the pilot's favourite aircraft whenever the family wished. The pilot was our best man and a very good friend.

There is a lovely, believable story about Freddie passing a DC10 ready to leave for America when he saw a little elderly lady coming down the steps in a panic. He stopped the car to find out what was wrong. She said she had taken fright while waiting in the big cabin. She had been saving for a year to visit her son, but suddenly felt she couldn't go through with it. He asked her would she feel better if he went with her. And he did so, happily abandoning his board meeting!

In the good old days when people didn't normally fly on Christmas Day, the story has it that a Laker flight with a plane load of live pigs had to divert from its destinations in eastern Europe due to fog on Christmas Eve. It managed to land and night stop in an adjacent country and then deliver its cargo safely on Christmas morning. On their delayed return to Gatwick the pilot and crew were met by Freddie with a magnum of Champagne!

Earlier on, when he became Managing Director of British United Airways, I had applied to him for a job while I was in Air Traffic Control. Instead of saying it wasn't their policy to employ women pilots, as BEA and BOAC had done, he wrote a courteous and encouraging letter.

Later, when my application to become a pilot with Morton's was accepted but then rescinded after a pilot had threatened to resign if I joined the company, the Press contacted several notable people including Sir Alan Cobham and Freddie Laker. I feel sure it was Freddie Laker who finally swayed the odds in my favour. I can just imagine him saying "For heaven's sake, give the girl back her job!"

Two years after he had founded his own airline, I had unbelievably become chairman of the British Air Line Pilots Association, B.A.L.P.A., Morton's local council – no-one else wanted the job! Towards the end of that year the British United pilots went on strike against a new personal contract their managing director wanted to impose on them as this contract would not give them the same safeguards as their B.A.L.P.A. one. I had to hold a meeting of the Morton's pilots to decide whether they would support them. It was not a success and when we descended into the pub below, Freddie bounded in from the opposite door, saying "Hello Luv, I bet you're the Chairman, the Secretary, the whole bloody lot!" I replied "I think I am going to need a job." He wasn't a union man, but also added that I would be welcome aboard Laker any time. As my sons continued to enjoy holidays in Menorca, we were very grateful to be able to fly with his airline when Dan-Air didn't have an aircraft going there.

Both sons had said they wanted to be pilots, but as they both had a slight sight defect, Dan-Air was unable to sponsor them. However, I had always said I didn't mind what they did – go to the moon, or deep sea diving, as long as they found something that satisfied them. Both have achieved different, but associated things – one on the artistic side, the other on the practical.

Having gone to Christ's Hospital, the Blue Coat School in Horsham, Jon went on to the Rose Bruford College of Speech and Drama, graduating with a diploma in stage management in 1974. He worked his way up with stage and pop stars like Elton John, becoming a freelance lighting designer in 1984. He specialised in conference product launches and live events. He lit the opening of the Eurotunnel and the new airport terminals at Stansted and Manchester, opened by Her Majesty The Queen and the Duke of Edinburgh. For the Millennium he was asked to light up London from Tower Bridge to Vauxhall Bridge, the Houses of Parliament and Big Ben. In the July he worked with Major Sir Michael Parker, lighting the Royal Military Tattoo and has carried on to light Military Benevolent events like 'Music On Fire'. As part of the Queen's Golden Jubilee celebrations he lit 'All The Queen's Horses' in Windsor Great Park with a cast of a thousand horses – very difficult to control – and has continued to design the lighting for many big events. How he designs and blends the wonderful variety in colours I do not know.

Chris, the practical one, went to the sister school, King Edward's in Witley. After trying a few things, he became a heating and ventilation engineer, working initially on a big new bank in London. He then worked in the Gatwick Hilton Hotel, following on with the old and new Air Traffic Control Towers on the airport, where he met some of the controllers who had worked with me and learned of some of my faux pas! He has continued with companies which specialise in the maintenance and safety of big buildings.

I am, of course, very proud of both of them.

As a pilot, one of my worst near faux pas and my most frightening experience happened at Newcastle due early winter snow. As we approached the airport we were told that the runway had been sanded and the braking was good. However, after landing I had to taxi to the end and use the turning circle off to one side. Instead of turning, the aircraft continued in a straight line towards the grass. All I could do was pray. My prayer was heard – and we stopped at the very edge! I inched the aircraft very slowly round and taxied gently down the runway to the parking area which I found, like the circle, was covered in ice. I curtly advised Air Traffic and our cabin crew that I would not allow the passengers to disembark until a pathway had been sanded to the terminal building. You can imagine what I said about the turning circle!

Newcastle again came into the picture when towards the end of August 1980 I did my so-called last flight for the benefit of the Press. Due to Miguel's deteriorating health, I had advised Dan-Air that I would be retiring in the September. A Press lunch had been arranged at the airport and before leaving the cockpit I was warned by Air Traffic not to forget my lipstick! Before I could attend, I was asked to take a phone call from the German Press. This took quite a long while so that they had to start without me. I quietly sat down in the nearest available seat, but suddenly, having been noticed, was taken to the top table. Afterwards I was interviewed by the British Press who kindly presented me with a huge rake, having heard that I was retiring to a market garden! I was flown back to Gatwick as a passenger and hate to admit that I left the rather long rake with my younger son, hoping he might use it.

In fact I did not retire for another two weeks and my last flight was to Menorca where Miguel's family presented us with an enormous 'ensaimada', a typical pastry cake, which we greatly enjoyed on our return to Gatwick, with something from the bar! The landing at Mahon, Menorca was my very last one as I let Mr. Wilson, the First Officer, fly us back. All I had ever wanted to do was fly and one thing led to another. I had never dreamt of being an airline pilot.

Having had some problems with Morton's, I was very lucky to have been accepted by Dan-Air. After having a Dakota wished on them through a bet, Davies and Newman, a big ship broking company, had formed Dan-Air in 1953 and it became the biggest independent British airline with the greatest number of different aircraft. It ended up with forty nine Comets, more than any other airline in the world, but before that had used the faithful Dakota as well as Dove, York, Bristol Freighter and Ambassador. The turbo-prop H.S. 748 and pure jet B.A.C. 1-11 came next, followed by the Boeing 707, 727, 737, Airbus A300 and smaller B.A.e. 146. With its variety of aircraft the Company was able to cope with big and small charters, several scheduled services and a great number of inclusive tour flights. The standard of training was very high and their engineering base at Lasham provided the overhaul and maintenance, not only of their own aircraft, but for other airlines too.

Despite its diversity, Dan-Air remained a family airline and, with very few exceptions, one knew that everyone would do their job as a team and to the best of their ability. It was incredibly sad that it was taken over in 1992 by British Airways. But the spirit of Dan-Air still lives on world-wide in the several hundred members of its Association and in the minds of the public.

Ironically, not having wanted me in the first place, I have become a retired British Airways Captain – and they now have many more women pilots!

Chapter 21

Retirement

Retirement in Menorca was the beginning of a completely different chapter, although aviation caught up with me briefly in the October of 1980 when I was invited to attend the British Airline Pilots Autumn Conference to receive their Silver Medal. I was deeply honoured, but Miguel's health had not improved sufficiently to make another journey. After apologising, I requested that the Medal be received on my behalf by the Dan-Air Pilots Chairman. It was given to me early in the New Year at a small ceremony at Mahon airport, kindly arranged by our Dan-Air agent, Margaret Thomas.

Happily, Miguel's health slowly improved and he only tended to develop bronchitis when we visited England. He had been through so much in the Spanish Civil War as a paramedic and afterwards he had had to patiently put up with my flying and the English climate. He was, however, a great companion with a similar sense of humour, love of beautiful scenery and music. Not being initially keen on flying, having had to fly low through bad weather to visit an infirm brother, he became quite happy with smooth jet flying above the clouds, and on a clear day was thrilled with a view of Mont Blanc and the beautiful panorama of the Swiss Alps.

Our new home slowly evolved to become the rambling farmhouse I had designed on a rough piece of paper. Our one-roomed cottage with its open car port had originally been built by Senor Ceferino, the market gardener. It had thick dry stone walls with tree trunks he had cut himself to support the roof. We did our best to follow on and blend in with the countryside.

On buying the land, we became one of seven associates with a share in a neighbour's well, but only our garden reservoir was fed from this. The cottage had relied on a shallow rain water tank into which roots had grown. Initially armed with plastic bottles we had to request drinking water from the village shop. A supply of clean water and an internal tank in the kitchen became very necessary. This was achieved with the use of a pneumatic drill to penetrate the hard base rock of Alcaufar. I was invited to inspect the progress. I happily agreed, not knowing what I was letting myself in for. I had to descend a rope ladder for the first time in my life. I decided it was too small. I only heard the next day that the pneumatic drill had been defeated and it had been decided to try a stick of dynamite. It didn't go off. Overnight it was thought that a second stick might do the trick. It did. They both went off together. When told, I imagined our little Perlita up at 30,000 feet! We did end up with a really big tank.

Anyone interested in market gardening that didn't have land of their own could be keen to work land with water available. Early on we were lucky enough to find someone happy to cultivate our long piece of land. He planted whatever he liked and then gave us a generous amount of the produce. Miguel was able to teach me some of his Mother's recipes which, together with the famous paella, were enjoyed by friends and family. Only once did I have to look after the land myself for six months. I did, however, concentrate on the flower garden and made the beds far too big. They required a lot of watering. Miguel escaped by saying that he was the engineer!

I also helped lay some crazy paving slabs on our front patio and, with permission from the land owner, helped our builder friend, Manolo, collect stones that had fallen from walls in abandoned fields near the sea. We would sally forth with rubber buckets and a wheelbarrow. After filling the car boot several times, it was felt that a lorry was really necessary! These stones were used to face the breeze block walls of our garage and blend in with the countryside.

Our artistic patio archways crowned with an individual decorative stone were also due to Manolo.

In between the ongoing work we would walk down to the cala (creek) for a lunchtime swim and a local gin on the rocks. Despite the chaos, visitors were always welcome. During quieter periods, we were able to see more of Miguel's warm and friendly family. They would check on our progress, and we enjoyed visiting them in their home in Alayor in the centre of the island as well as at their attractive weekend/holiday house on the southern coast. Situated on a sloping hill, it has a wonderful view of the sea and sandy beaches. My family, faithful to Menorca, also enjoyed the adjacent long beach of Son Bou when on holiday. It had several attractions including a surprising maze and twisting water chutes. I tried videoing their descent but the camera went walk-about!

On other occasions we also enjoyed joining friends for a picnic on an unspoilt beach in the north of the island where one could stand vertically with hands by one's sides and not topple over in the deep buoyant water, and swim in the peace and tranquillity of a big open horseshoe bay.

Visitors interested in more than sun, sea and sandy beaches are able to find many archaeological ancient remains. As one of the Balearic Islands, Menorca is steeped in history dating back to the Bronze Age. It has been invaded and used by many nationalities including Arabic and Western, ending up with French, English and Catalan Spanish. It has only one mountain in the middle of the island, which is just over a 1,000 feet high and is crowned by a monastery and a Cross of Christ.

Persuaded by Miguel's family, we met up early one cool and misty 5th of November and climbed the winding hairpin road to the top of Monte Toro. The sun came out halfway up and we were able to see some of the beautiful bays and creeks emerging from the mist. When we reached the top it was still hazy, but we were able to see more of the island. On a clear day one could have a wonderful view of almost all of the island, including the old and new airports. Miguel's nephew and his bride were indeed married some years later in the ancient little Monastery church.

Despite, or perhaps because of being subjected to invasion, hunger and civil war, Menorceans are resilient, hard-working, caring and friendly. Before tourism, there was little unemployment. Apart from fishing and farming, one of the main industries is the making of shoes and boots, which are sold to Europe and America. I still have a beautiful pair of boots. They also know how to celebrate their fiestas.

Every summer each town and village celebrates its own fiesta. Even little Alcaufar had visiting young drum majorettes and competitions for the children. The adults had a football match on the beach, a short service in the small chapel (where we were married) in the afternoon, and in the evening everyone enjoyed a really good professional firework display staged on the other side of the creek. It was started by a big bonfire lit on the flat 'aircraft carrier' rock at the entrance to the creek. The rock and the long ridge opposite with its Martello Tower would then be outlined by the lighting of little paraffin flares, for which the young people had spent many days collecting tins. The fiesta was rounded off with a dance under the stars. The bigger towns and cities had fairgrounds and traditional medieval displays by the special Island horses and their elegant riders, which were unique to Menorca. The firework display across the water to Mahon harbour was indeed always spectacular.

The long winding approach with its deep-water channel to the harbour had always been greatly valued by so many, including Admiral Lord Nelson. During the 1990s we were invited aboard a modern British Naval ship and, when requested, I was shown their impressive radar control room, bringing back many memories.

We returned to England for many Christmases and also family events, good and bad. The happy ones were the marriage of younger son Chris to Liz, and the birth of Lewis, Jon's son, brother to four year old Samantha. The bad ones were due to accidents and serious illnesses. When we heard that Jon had been badly injured when scaffolding had collapsed, we left within two hours. Thanks goodness, with time and physiotherapy, he recovered completely. We also spent time with my dear step-mother, Nan, when she was dying. I was very sad to lose her but knew that she was then free to continue. I was only pleased that she had seen the Perlita finished and was happy for us. Despite her flair for renovation and interior decoration, she hadn't been able to imagine what we could do with our one-roomed Casita!

Sometime later, in 1989, we had to return to England again when an aunt had had a car accident. While there I was suddenly taken to hospital after a 'malicious' tumour made itself known. I was saved by a phone call from a caring friend, Jean Whittow, and a great surgeon. Jon was initially working out of the country, but Chris came every evening and then went on to see our aunt who had been hospitalised. Ironically, I was sent to her hospital for a week's convalescence and crossed overnight with her before she was discharged. Miguel and I were then invited to stay with our incredible friends Jock and Betty Hunter. Jock had become my mentor from the time I had struggled to become a commercial pilot and there had always been a warm welcome from Betty. They put up with us for several weeks after my two operations. I was glad to have introduced them to Menorca and to be able to share many happy holidays with them.

On returning to Menorca, I was greatly helped by Miguel and Magdalena Mercadal. She did most of the housework, and we have remained firm friends. As she loved animals, she would also caringly look after our cats while we were away.

When we retired we had been adopted by cats and ended up with four. They each had their own bunk beds. We liked dogs as well but couldn't have them because our garden walls were too low. One of our big cats actually puffed himself up and saw off two escapee long-haired Alsatians.

Other friends who helped were Frank and Nancy Cox. Nancy had introduced me to the Air Safety Group in London and Frank was a retired but gifted Air Force and airline captain.

Menorca lends itself to being painted and I have many water colours painted by Frank, the most ethereal being 'Moonlight in Menorca', bathing a hamlet on a hill in light, which I unbelievably saw one evening. On retiring, they had bought Casita Teresa from my step-mother, Nan, but had found it too small when all their family joined them. We were able to buy it back from them and let it to friends and airline people, making up a little for our early retirement. In turn we also had to sell it to complete our Perlita. I was very sad to do so but I couldn't cope with both. However, Frank's pictures bring back many special memories.

On one of our return flights from England the captain was the Dan-Air Chief Pilot. When I asked him how many women pilots they had, he said he didn't know because British Airways kept poaching them! Sadly Dan-Air was taken over by British Airways shortly afterwards but we were able to fly back to attend a wonderful get-together of over 1,000 people in a hangar at Gatwick which showed that the Dan-Air spirit would survive.

Happily, Miguel was able to survive to enjoy many extra years in the island home he loved before he died in 1999. I returned to live in England in 2000 to be near my sons and family, but still keep in touch with Miguel's warm and caring family. I was finally able to sell the Perlita to an Englishman, Bob Foster, who had always wanted some agricultural land – and liked the cats. I wouldn't have sold it to anyone who didn't! He has been kept happy renovating our rambling farmhouse, and the cats have kept him company.

....

I am now able to see more of my grand-daughter, Samantha, who as a Captain in the Army served in Iraq and Afghanistan, and is the mother of my long and strong great-grandson, Monty. I can also catch up with his uncle, my grandson Lewis, who has bravely faced cancer and who is now continuing in his father Jon's footsteps into the lighting industry. Lewis proves the adage that 'it doesn't matter what happens to you, it's how you cope with it'. He has coped amazingly well and is now in remission.

I am so proud of all my family and thankful that I was able to do the job I loved and fulfil my need to fly. When I look up at the contrails in the sky, I think 'I used to make them ...'